CREATURES OF ART WHO BREATHE POETRY

AF239950

EVERGREEN DIARY

EVERGREEN DIARY

Contents

Acknowledgements   *xix*

Prologue   *xxi*

1. Dialectical   1

2. Definition Of Love   3

3. About The Writer   5

—

4. A Letter To Ares From Aphrodite//in Another Life   9

5. The Call Of Elpis   11

6. 3:33 Am   14

7. 12:28 Am   16

8. You   18

9. How Did You Know It Was Love?   20

10. Moon   21

11. Why   22

12. Shirt Sleeve   23

13. About The Writer   25

—

14. Hey   29

15. Empty   30

16. About The Writer   32

—

17. Far From Home   35

18. Tangled   37

19. Empty   39

Contents

20. About The Writer   41

—

21. Truths I Felt   45

22. Dear Self   46

23. Christmas   47

24. About The Writer   49

—

25. November Yearnings   53

26. Forbidden   55

27. Unfinished   56

28. Your Name   58

29. Baby's Love Song   60

30. I Love You In Colours   62

31. When I'm In Love with You   64

32. About The Writer   66

—

33. A Letter To My 15 Year Old Self   69

34. Break Me Again   75

35. Our If's And Parents   78

36. About The Writer   80

—

37. Dreaming   83

38. I Am Human   84

39. Keep Hoping   85

Contents

40.	She	86
41.	Butterflies	87
42.	Diamond	88
43.	About The Writer	89
44.	Dandelion	93
45.	To An Online Friend Who Is Closer Than My Real Life Friend	95
46.	Nightfall	97
47.	Just Like You Do	98
48.	Waves	100
49.	About The Writer	101
50.	The River Called	105
51.	Sakura And You	107
52.	About The Writer	109
53.	My Soul	113
54.	Where The Darkness Resides	114
55.	Our Summer	115
56.	About The Writer	116
57.	Will You Cry When I Die	119
58.	A Lover Like No Other	122

Contents

59. Beauty Lies Within 125

60. About The Writer 128

—

61. Khuli Kitaab 131

62. Sach Hai Ya Nahi 132

63. An Open Letter To Phoebe Buffay 133

64. About The Writer 135

—

65. Dear Heart, You Know It All 139

66. A List Of Things I Want You To Do For Me After I'm 141
Gone

67. To The Deleted Selfie 143

68. Him And Hope 145

69. To The Boy Who Reminds Me Of Me 147

70. Yeh Khula Aasman, Aagaye Hum Kahan 149

71. On Holding On To Your Younger Self 151

72. About The Writer 153

—

73. A Familiar Stranger 157

74. The Cracked Vase 159

75. A Help From You To Yourself 161

76. Stormy Silence 163

77. Void 164

78. About The Writer 166

Contents

–

79. An Immortal Life	169
80. The Echo Within You	171
81. Homemaker: The Flightless Dove	172
82. The Naked Truth Of Lie	174
83. My Father: A Bliss To Me	176
84. About The Writer	178

–

85. To Loose A Beloved	181
86. Waning Light	182
87. Dandelions	183
88. The Ghost	184
89. Moving	186
90. About The Writer	187

–

91. Tell Me This Is Real And We Are Forever	191
92. A Letter To My 15-year-old Self	192
93. Paathu	195
94. What If's Of An Overthinker	198
95. About The Writer	199

–

96. So Close And Yet So Far	203
97. Post Its	207
98. Halfway There	211

Contents

99. About The Writer   215

—

100. I Say I Write   219

101. Perfections And Flaws   221

102. They Asked Me To Write Poetry   222

103. Love Taught Me   224

104. About The Writer   226

—

105. The Perfect Painting   229

106. Stars Of Kindness Shine The Brightest   231

107. Magic   233

108. Because I'll Love You   234

109. Realisations   235

110. About The Writer   236

—

111. Cadaver   239

112. Privilege   241

113. An Open Letter To My Younger Brother Of 8   243

114. About The Writer   245

—

115. At Night   249

116. Break Apart   250

117. Portrait Of A Lady   252

118. About The Writer   253

Contents

–

119. The Homesick Window   257

120. Maudlin Moon   258

121. Chapter 121   259

122. About The Writer   260

–

123. The Night Is Hunting   265

124. Ruka Ruka Sa Vaqt Hai   266

125. About The Writer   268

–

126. The Life Sailor   271

127. A Smile I Am   273

128. About The Writer   275

–

129. The World Is A Masquerade   279

130. Life   280

131. About The Writer   281

–

132. Dear Younger Self   285

133. Wo Pehli Baarish   287

134. The Girl At The Shore   288

135. About The Writer   290

–

136. My Eulogy To Myself :   293

Contents

137. The One That Got Away   295

138. Loving You Is Like   297

139. About The Writer   299

—

140. Wrong Routes   303

141. Nostalgia   305

142. About The Writer   308

—

143. Wallflower   311

144. I Told The Stars About You   312

145. About The Writer   314

—

146. Reasons   317

147. Comfort   320

148. Tales   322

149. About The Writer   325

—

150. Call Of The Blue   329

151. Mystery   331

152. A Lifetime Per Day   332

153. Healing Hurts   334

154. About The Writer   340

—

155. The Spirits Of The Lonely Graveyard   343

Contents

156. Words Do Wonders   345

157. About The Writer   346

158. Silly Maze   347

159. Crazy Love   350

160. A Walk In The Woods   351

161. Losing The Moonlight   353

162. About The Writer   354

_

163. Opportunity   357

164. One Last Time   359

165. About The Writer   360

_

166. Maybe   363

167. I've Seen People Hide Their Cowardice Under The Sheets Of Melancholy   365

168. The Epiphany Of My Alter Ego   367

169. I Can Just Dream Of You   369

170. Letting Go   372

171. About The Writer   374

_

172. Love Letters To Bombay And A Sporadic Lover   377

173. About The Writer   379

_

174. From Where It Fell Apart   383

Contents

175. Confessions   384

176. The Downfall   385

177. About The Writer   386

—

178. Girl At The Harbor   389

179. Pain Is A Synonym Of Disease   391

180. Loving Hard Sometimes   392

181. About The Writer   393

—

182. Metanoia   397

183. Déjà Vu   399

184. Heart: An Enchanter   400

185. Moonshine Blues   401

186. Golden Rain Shower   403

187. About The Writer   404

—

188. Broken   407

189. Perfect   408

190. It's Okay Not To Be Okay   409

191. Ghost   411

192. Buried   412

193. About The Writer   413

—

194. I Tend To Live In Parts   417

Contents

195. Run Away 418

196. There Were Grasses 419

197. About The Writer 420

–

198. Tum Ho 423

199. Kagaz Par Shor 424

200. Rakh Hona Chahata Hoon 425

201. About The Writer 426

–

202. Of Goodbyes 429

203. The Fault In Our Stars 432

204. Mulaqat 433

205. Phases Of The Moon 435

206. About The Writer 436

–

207. An Open Letter To The Person Who Would Like To 439
Pen Down Our Story

208. Mould 441

209. 3:00 A.m. 443

210. About The Writer 445

–

211. How I Fell In Love With Grief 449

212. I Still Draw Your Portaits 451

213. 4 Spring Passed 453

Contents

214. Mum Do You Know?   455

215. About The Writer   456

—

216. Hero-lovers   459

217. Fall   461

218. Satan Wears Red Lipstick   462

219. About The Writer   463

—

220. // Info //   467

Creatures of Art who breathe poetry

The special edition of 2021 featured with over 40+ writers. Thank you to all your contribution.

Acknowledgements

To all the selected writers, thankyou for being a part of this journey. To all who joined the anthology from the beginning and close to the deadline, your excitement and enthusiasm is much appreciated.

To the selection committee and the editorial team, your invaluable help made this anthology possible.

Prologue

Anthology is a sub section of Literature that comprises of works of various authors. Ever since the 17th century, anthology has been revolutionised by various people. Since it's a part of Literature, anthology book covers are always similar to poetry books and that's something I find very beautiful.

But I fear it has lost its meaning in the past few years, including the researched articles as a part of anthology and other pieces that aren't a part of this genre. This has raised a question of what does anthology include in today's world?

The answer is simple, it will always contain old and newly introduced forms of literature pieces: poems, short stories and open letters (and maybe more to come in the future). Anthology belongs to literature and it always will have a permanent place in it till the end of time. The authors selected for this edition were wonderful to work with, they are the writers worthy of their titles.

1. Dialectical

Lately people have been asking asking me, "What are you thinking?"
And I say "oh nothing" but what I actually want to say is about the chaos in this beautiful overworking organ called brain.
Why beautiful ? cause it's one thing I am proud of, one thing I can confidently gloat about. One thing where I don't have to constantly worry if I am good enough.
Why overworking ? because it doesn't stop with the overburdening thoughts that create a cacophony in my head.
From the moment my eyes wake up to the moment they close they are there like a constant reminder of my insecurities, my demons, all my decisions, my twisted relationships
and existential questions.
I am tired of their constant presence, too scared to face them and delve deep in the pit of doom again, too coward to acknowledge them, so I do what every coward does- Run.
Every person has their own mechanism of running.
Some start stress eating,
Some go stress shopping,
Some pretend that nothings happening,
My mechanism is that I overwork my body so much that this poor brain has no time to solve the crosswords of thoughts

swimming like a whirlpool in my head. Yes I'm running away but I like it. This futile try of running away every week. I am happy away from them but life is so ironic that it loves to bring me face to face with my thoughts over and over again.

The same journey all over again. The trigger, the helplessness, the bitter words, the constant criticizing my self worth, the weariness, the silent gut wrenching cries, the realization of being alone fighting battles, the pit of doom and finally I give up......give up to my thoughts and then come the days of ignoring myself like a plague. People avoid their ex and I avoid myself. Days pass without dates. When nothing matters. No one matters. No one to impress. A body without the heart.

Then I relapse back..In just a snap I'm back to beating hearts and happy smiles when I hear my favourite song remembering how I swayed my hips to it or I achieve something and make myself proud of the way I battled, or something simple like a stranger asked me how was my day today . Realization hits me like a truck of caffeine on a late night and I think what have I been mourning about all this while ? I have this beautiful life that I want to live. I want to feel once again that I'm alive. I want to count the stars under the open sky, run a race to the door, watch people passing by and hear songs that remind me of forgotten memories. But not many days pass by and someone asks me again what are you thinking about ? And again I say "oh nothing"

- Kamakshi Sardesai

2. Definition of love

Have you ever fallen in love ? They asked
I said I did with a coffee eyed young boy with a cute dimpled
smile which reached his ears on seeing pineapple pizzas.

How did you know it was love ? They asked
I said it was simple he made me laugh on my rainiest days and
smelt like my every dream come true.

How did you tell him you loved him? They asked
I told him every day when I missed something important in
my life just to listen to him rant about his day,
when I looked at him with heart eyes or when I interlaced our
fingers at every chance I received.

What did he say? They asked
Nothing as he could never interpret my language of love I
said. His language of love had words while mine were little
perennial actions.

Did he ever love you? They asked
Maybe he did or maybe he didn't but even if he did his heart
had never learnt to listen and mine was afraid to speak. His
love was like a mirage,

I could see it but could never feel its presence.

Why didn't you guys work out ? They asked
Because we had different definitions of love I said. He was the carefree, adventurous type that needed a bold heart who dared him to live every day.

What is your definition of love? They asked
Love is where all my spoken and unspoken words are heard, a place where my cons are loved and not just accepted, a place that I want to call home.

Do you still believe in love? they asked
I said I do but it might not have the same definition for me as others.

- Kamakshi Sardesai

3. About the writer

About the writer:

Kamakshi Sardesai

Kamakshi is happily introvert except when high on adrenaline. 24/7 dreamer. Die hard rom com fan. But murder mysteries are her jam. Usually found high on caffeine. She is a writer, youtuber, dancer and a frequent user of sarcasm.

4. a letter to ares from aphrodite//in another life

my hands are shaking as i write my thoughts
im too tipsy,
shouldn't drink that much,
but i couldn't stop myself from pouring it all

am i drowning my sorrows?
i'll let you decide
there's music playing, i don't know the song,
don't know what it is that reminds me of you

in another life,
i'll be your girl,
we'll keep all our promises,
be us against the world
in another life,
i will make us stay
so we don't have to say we were the ones that got away,
the ones that got away

i didn't even try to think of you,
but you came in my mind like the lord you are,
sometimes it feels like im being watched by you,

i remember the time we both met,
when i was nervous and you loved the way i was,
hesitantly i hugged you but you didn't let me go

in another life,
i'll be your boy,
i'll get better and will stand beside you,
in another life,
we will make us stay
so we don't have to say we were the ones that got away,
the ones that got away

i open my eyes and i see you crying with me,
in my dreams, i see you kissing me,
in poetry, i see you smiling at me,
now i'll drown myself in your love,
cause in another life,
i will be your love,
you'll kiss my mind and I'll kiss you on your heart,
in another life,
we will stay together always and forever,
we won't let go,
we won't let go.

- muski

5. the call of elpis

sometimes, i feel like drowning,
others, i feel like saving myself, just riding the waves,
desperately holding on to the weeds,
my feet digging in the sand,
my mind forcing me to not jump in the water,
but suddenly im going under,
the earth beneath opens up and swallows me whole,
i hear someone call my name, it's elpis,
she takes my hand in hers,
we walk through the water
there, appears a cottage,
covered with hyacinths, daisies, violets, crocuses and irises,
she tells me to look inside,
through the boarded window,
i was looking at someone's back, they turn around as if
someone called out their name,
i gasp in surprise, it was me, but a bit older,
she's cooking for the three people seated at the table, i can't see
their faces,
then he looks right into my eyes, i panic and hide,
they call out my name,
now i can see everyone,
it's them,

the lover is standing beside her, aimlessly kissing their head,
the wife and the sister sitting,
all of them smiling but still looking at me with yearning eyes,
elpis puts her hand on my eyes,
images drift by,
are these flashbacks? no, it's the future,
laughing at the kitchen table, card games in the lounge,
teaching at the local library,
poetry readings,
them,
elpis softly reminds me "blood of the covenant is thicker than
the water of the womb"
she now holds me, i open my eyes and everything is gone,
im no longer under water,
i cry out for them,
elpis silences me "they're still going to be there, child. it's upto
you now,
do you want to drown in the turbulent waves of the water of
the womb?"
no i don't,
i will hold on, even if the weeds give up and snap, i will hold
on,
i will hold on to see that sunrise with them,
to see the moonrise too,
we're bound by blood, melancholy, anger and love,
now, with our tears, sedum and protea will bloom
everlastingly

- muski

6. 3:33 AM

someone who looks like you,

who might that be,

the different sides of yourself?

the friend you have been together for more than sixteen years,

molded into each other?

your lover?

a stranger?

what will you do if you find your doppelgänger? would you

go and say hi?

would you apologize to them?

would they even understand why?

i think i would just stare,

analysing all of the small details,

the nose, the eyes, the smile,

maybe then i would realise that it isn't bad to be me,

maybe then i would finally understand why my lover looks at

me like i am a god,

maybe i would finally understand the look in my friend's eyes

that is always so thankful,

thank you for being my friend, she lets me know,

maybe then i would finally understand what it is to not hate

myself

- muski

7. 12:28 AM

a lot of people might already be asleep
i should be too
i want to but i can't
the thoughts won't stop running,
every time i think i have them in my grip, they slip away,
sitting on my bed with my knees pulled to my chest
head resting on them,
what happened to me?
why did it all turn out like this?
it isn't my fault i know
sometimes i get lost in the mirage of my disappointments
not a fool for expecting
not a fool for accepting
not a fool for loving

go to sleep at an unreasonable hour because you can't stop crying or you cry so much that you pass out, have nightmares, try to sleep again, wake up, don't feel like eating but have to, eat enough, try to work, try to stay happy, try to stay focused, try to not dwell on certain things, watch random videos on your phone, evening rolls in, listen to music, dinner time, again no appetite, but still eat, sometimes you do feel hungry and eat well, admire the food babie after, talk to that special someone about the said food babie, let them appreciate you,

feel like crying when they compliment you, when they tell you that they're proud of you because all your younger self wanted was to hear these things
if he had, none of this would have happened

- muski

8. you

i feel nothing and everything at the same time

i want to cry but no tears come out

i want to be beside you,

you to hug me,

piece me back together,

but that's just a fantasy, right?

the one that got away,

that's how you'll be known.

got away because you got pushed.

i tried,

tried so hard to find someone who could make me feel like you do

make me feel human again,

what did i even expect?

there is only one you.

i need you,

i don't know if i should,

the walls of my bedroom have seen everything,

the pillows know who i pretend they are when i hug them at night,

all i want is you,

just you,

because i can never replace you.

- muski

9. how did you know it was love?

it was quite simple for me to realise that what i felt for him, was indeed love.

it was when the image in my head after reading my own poem was just his face,

the lines of my poetry being the lines on his face; the laugh lines, the way his brows furrow in worry,

the sweet words that flow easily out my heart being the honey that drips from his lips,

the warmth that i feel while reading poetry being the warmest of hugs i have ever experienced by just looking into his eyes,

the yearning, the pang in my heart which i used to feel like reading poetry is not there anymore because i gave away my heart to him.

- muski

10. moon

tonight, i lay down under the dark eerie sky
the only light is coming from her, the moon
she stands over me, protecting my heart from the cruel world
i long to touch her,
to be held in her arms like a long lost lover.

- muski

11. why

you always had a grip on my weak heart,
and
you have always had the power to crush it,
but you didn't,
that still haunts me
why didn't you?

- muski

12. shirt sleeve

[shirt sleeve]
holding on to a parent's shirt sleeve in a crowded area
trusting them
them protecting you
i didn't have that privilege
I'll be the guiding light for my younger self
hold on to me, little one
[shirt sleeve]
it is in human nature to hold on to someone you trust in unfamiliar situations,
kids desperately cling on to their parents shirt sleeves in crowded places,
they know they are protected, they put that trust in their parents
i never had that privilege of knowing that no matter what, I'll be protected,
i held on to my own shirt,
it got torn sometimes,
sometimes i tore it myself,
to cover the bleeding heart on my sleeve,
now i feel someone tugging at my shirt,
it's me,
my younger self,

they're crying,

i bend down, pick her up,

slowly running my hands through his hair,

"hold on to me, little one"

i run as fast as i can through the storm of unfamiliarity, of regret, of guilt, of despair,

she's holding on to my shirt sleeve and i won't let him go.

- muski

13. About the writer

<u>About the writer:</u>

All poets are sick and muski is no exception. she has been
seen having the blood pumping organ instead of eyes when
talking about literature, you know, like a nerd. muski has
found peace in the yearned chaos, writing about her
unnamed muse who they describe as ethereal but deadly,
while her coffee's getting cold and the classical music
accompanies the moon.

14. Hey

Death. It never did really scared me. But now, I'm scared. It is scary to know that my story will end, it's scary to know that my existence will be forgotten. It is scary to know that my space shall be replaced. I'm scared that the mission I came with may remain incomplete but I am happy to know that with this and complete task they might send me again to write a news story with the New task.

- Akihi

15. Empty

Without even saying goodbye,
Without even saying why
You left me in the house
filled with void.
Yesterday we walked on the roads
where you and I created memories
and now I am here alone
with your empty space.
You said on memories last forever
and nobody can take it away,
but you are wrong my love,
it's is fading away.
What will I do with these memories?
What will I do with this empty space of yours? What will I do
with the voice of yours screaming in my head?
What will I do with the smell of yours touching my soul?
Now here I am!
walking through a empty lanes,
sitting at a empty place,
gazing at our empty sky,
and feeling your empty space.
What will I do with this memory?
which keeps reminding me your eyes

The pain that you carried,
clenches my throat and
tears my soul apart.
I can't say you goodbye and
I can't let you go and
I can't forgive you for leaving me
with an empty space of yours!

- Akihi

16. About the writer

About the writer:

Disha Chowdhury

Akihi is a pen name she gave herself which means a phase of conversation where even after asking for direction, a person forgets about it. She wants to explore every field on her way. Though she is new to the writing field, but she believes that she is able to show her readers the direction to tranquility.

17. Far from home

"Same room,
same insanity,
similar locks,
similar keys"

.

I have heard the story before,
even felt it,
I know beginning
I know the end
Still the hooked parts
feel like moments
to live for

.

Twisted tales
takes a ...
a lot of strength,
as so you know
the locks remain
still in the end

.

view so significant
to be captured in,

still the stories
brings about sin

.

Edges dried up
an ocean so filled,
life is a ... sweet sin

.

Visitors come
visitors go
the stories remain
alive within.

- Bhawna Saini

18. Tangled

So many emotions
that we feel,
some are hard to express
others we show with ease,

.

one such emotion is sadness,
it be may be the weakness that
keeps rushing back with the
memories or the guilt of not
being able to face it all alone

.

sometimes we are not able
to solve some puzzles,
other times we might even
solve them but the picture
we get isn't the same we want,

.

there's a lot that we know about
right and wrong but
the heart feels ...
what it feels right
and the way it sink
with every beat we feel...

we feel the hard emotions
deep inside us ... lost in
different corners ...
dark ones,

.

permit those dark sides
to see the rays of light,
don't lose the hopes...
take your time and
when it feels right...
allow yourself to see
the dawn after the
darkest night.

- Bhawna Saini

19. Empty

A grief, more of bloodbath
a pain, smelling stinky dark
a sorrow, say it's the base line path
.

you saw me,
like none of those who I had
like no one who so ever tried, no one wanted to so much that
it is so soft and so wise
.

the pretty stars on the roadside ride,
the seat and cushion cover vibe,
it is the best memory that makes me wonder had I felt before
more divine?
.

an emptiness in stomach aches
a mind full of sights
a dream I want to chase
a past creating my demise
.

you read my thoughts
it feels so warm yet so cold,
freezes the beats which
catches me all along,

I know what it is like what you go though,
believe me it isn't easy the road
which we belong to

.

a box inside
very bright/shiny/sweet and sunrise

.

a box out
broken/tired stories/others had and fear nights

.

heart knows it is right,
mind never allows thee,
whispering noises
which says you heard stories where
hurt will stay the same
and it keeps getting loud when you allowed-
believe me
it isn't worth the game
it isn't worth the game!

- Bhawna Saini

20. About the writer

<u>About the writer:</u>

Bhawna Saini

Bhawna being a passionate writer tries to gather her thoughts based on the different events of her life, loves to explore new things, create new pages and fill new colors of rainbow in the clouds of her imagination.

21. Truths I felt

- Fear of failure is way more dangerous than failure itself

-Future is imagination
past is a memory
but don't take a long walk down these lanes
for they both may cause the present some serious injury

- World never sees the preparation
for its too boring to watch
all they look at is the result
and then wonder how you got it all

- Self sufficient soul suffers seldom

- Stop expecting, start embracing
- Prashansa Bharti

22. Dear self

DEAR SELF,

I know that I have done a lot of harm to you(especially mentally). It's been tough for everyone out there and you are no different so take it easy on yourself. Give yourself some breaks from distress, depression, guilt, remorse and all those negative nagging feelings that are weighing you down. Move that burden once a while off your shoulder and them slowly learn to remove them from your life permanently. Friends or no friends, mental battles need to be fought alone, for its a fight with self not with the world. So here's an advice I know it's hard but hang in there, you are tougher than these problems. I know I can't repair the damages I have done to you, however I can try to nurse you back to health with best of my efforts and will power.

This might sound stupid but advices can be given by many but noone can put them to use for you. So start walking on the path ahead , for people may remove thorns and pebbles from your path but they themselves cannot walk down that path for you.

- Prashansa Bharti

23. Christmas

Vacations are here,
so is happiness.
Relatives will be coming
with a box of chocolates.

The aura of happiness
can be easily felt,
by the Christmas trees and decorations,
by the chocolate cookie smell.

Everything seems so joyful
that every child forgets,
the school will soon reopen
with teachers demanding for projects.

Forgetting the pain for a few days
children engross themselves
in celebrating and decorating
waiting for the harness bells.

Finally, when the table set,
when holy tree glows the brightest
children reach the peak of merriness

receive the gifts that they had expect.

- Prashansa Bharti

24. About the writer

<u>About the writer:</u>

Prashansa Bharti

She is a wanderlust who roams in the streets of her memory lane and imagination in the infinite universe of her own. Feelings are her weakness which she tackles with the help of pen and paper.

25. November yearnings

Oh November, the month when in the morning she wakes up with her cheeks resembling the hues of Rubellite and he goes back to sleep cozily after tucking her inside the blanket with him.

In this blustery half spent November, I yearn for you to shorten the spaces between us.

I wanna feel the gratitude that you feel after waking up from a nightmare, out of breath in the middle of your sleep, and realizing that life is different but so much better.

I wanna feel the contentment that a poetess perceives when she fills the incomplete verses of her poetry and has the urge to read it again and again because it's something she's never done and now she believes she's written something as alluring as her muse.

Our worlds might be too far and dissimilar but the universe we choose over and over again in each other's warmth is brighter and warmer just like the first glint of sun that makes its way from the window to my room on an invigorating November morning, just like a bittersweet coffee slipping through the tongue and soothing all the taste buds.

Tell me, how would you feel when one day maybe on a crisp November morning you'll wake up from your sleep next to me, surpassing all the spaces between us.

- Rani Hirani

26. Forbidden

I didn't hear anything against you, I chose not to listen,

Now I'm a homeless wolf that all the forests have forbidden.

You used my vehemence to get over your hurt,

I use your indifference to write my poetry.

In these verses I'll bleed forever

from the places of my skin I could never cut.

I'll keep scribbling you until the day I no longer feel any emotion,

Until the day my poetry looses its metaphor and personification.

I still can't hear anything against you, I'll never listen.

You'll always be my home out of all places forbidden.

- Rani Hirani

27. Unfinished

In giving what you want I forget my needs
Pleading you to stay, I'm on my knees.
But again, you leave me like an unfinished novel,
Forgetting it was written for you.

You said you want to share home with me,
Travel to all the sacred places with me,
Dance on the Taylor's songs with me,
With me, but why you are never with me-

On the nights when I try choking myself,
On the nights when it is harder to breathe,
On the nights when I'm shattered and cry myself to sleep.

Why the questions you once used to answer
are now ignored with grumpy shrugs?
Screaming that I'm not here forever
You wake up high on your drugs.

And me? Oh, I find my way back to some unaddressed letters.
That I can't express or show to no one.
If my skin was a paper, it'd be a masterpiece dedicated to you.
Engraved your name in the ink of blue.

Honey, if you leave and miss me,

You can try writing me back and meet in the universe where

you care about my needs,

In the times when I don't have to beg on my knees,

In the city where you share home with me,

In the nights when you are there with me,

Forever with me.

- Rani Hirani

28. Your name

I blushed under your red hoodie
as I felt your fingers tracing my neck
making me wear a vintage chain
with the initial of your name.
Damn your pretty name.

We again rendezvoused at a place that you chose.
Oh, I still have got that rose,
tucked somewhere in the pages of my diary.
But like us, its fragrance is gone.
Look the time has changed everything
Faded are your feelings just like a lost spring.
Cherry on top, my best friend has turned mean.
Lord, tell me what does this mean.

To make the promises that always get broken,
Some words are better unspoken
But words don't decide to be the lie.
Oh your pretty lies.
A home to all my butterflies.
Where my heart got flattered
Now it's manipulated and shattered.
Someone please tell me, what does it mean?

To call it love when it's something else.

To be in love when you're loosing yourself.

I cry under my red sweater

Feeling heaviness inside my neck

Giving you back your vintage chain

Because now I'm erasing your name.

Oh, what is your name?

Screw your pretty name.

- Rani Hirani

29. Baby's love song

My baby says she'll stay forever
But does she know that she should know people can leave
whenever?
At any time, at any moment.
Cause this is life, nothing permanent.
So today I'll tell her to write me a written piece.
In the corner of which I can find my peace.
When I'll be shattered,
numb, maybe cold hearted.
When I'll lose my sanity,
Crying in the shower solely.
Cursing the word infinity,
Despaired from love, fully.

My baby says she'll stay forever
But does she know that she should know
people can leave whenever?
So maybe write a letter?
I'll keep it forever.
And I'll know,
Forever know that you loved me somewhere.
Even if it was for a while, for a moment.
Love is gone but pain is permanent.

- Rani Hirani

30. I love you in colours

When you see the additive of all the colors, it's white.
And black is the result when all the colors get absorbed in one.
Through ends of black and white
Above the definitions of wrong and right, in all the colors, I love you.

Brown- I'll pour love in your tea oh no, coffee and press my lips tenderly on your forehead. My arms will always be open for you, there for you to hold you as tight as they can because all I ever want to be is a safe embrace where you can reveal all your abashes and vexations and go to bed with a little smile on your face. Depending on someone can be good or bad but, in your presence, I find wholesomeness, a hug that is deeper than the surface, a love that surpasses everything.

Grey-
All the mornings when you wake up with uncertainty, numb and blank cause you've felt too much and now it's grey, all faded.
In your victories I celebrate with you,
But when you cry, my heart aches too.
I want to remind you the value of your sheer existence. Trust me when I say, you give me the meaning that I was always

searching for.

It's not about our love, it's not about the crazy friendship, it's something that makes you the muse to my ink and words.

Blue-

A soul that reflects the hues of sapphire,

You once were an unsolved mystery, now you're an ocean in which I've deeply diven.

I'll never stop falling, I just can't.

The heaviness that you carry inside your heart, please share with me the weight of it.

Hold my head against your chest and let me kiss it.

Red-

Passionate as the flames of fire, you're a devil that even angels would fall for. How do you suffer so much yet fight back stronger and put your head up in grace?

The warmth of your palm melts my iciness. I can't give you the blood that you bled in your wars but to all your scars, I'll kiss them better. Fools are the ones who let you go, to me your absence is brutal than the atrocities of this world.

- Rani Hirani

31. When I'm in love with you

If I'm in love with you, take me to your favorite places, tell me your favorite poetry, fill me in with the traits of the fictional characters that you admire, talk for hours, and lay with me under the starry sky. I'll love it, all of it because even though I don't know every detail of yours, I would love to.

If I'm in love with you, be sure that I'm loving every piece of you and know that your existence is the air I breathe in.

If I am in love with you, correct me when I'm wrong, tell me what you hate, take your time, do everything, but never doubt it.

Because-

When I'm in love with you, I breathe you.

I paint your name in the sky, sit on my terrace, and sky-gaze for hours. feeling lighter and feeling more in love with every blow of the evening breeze. when thunder screams in my sky and all the bridges i built start burning, you tell me i have you. perhaps that's why you got the thunder blue eyes.

When I'm in love with you, I ink you.

I'm a writer and I write about so many things but every time I hold my pen with your thoughts in my head, I scribble love on the pages, and at that time I'm nothing but a lover. A lover who wishes to put in the words the power of affection, who wishes to portray the beauty of emotions that my heart is overwhelmed it.

When I'm in love with you, I worship you.
A heart that is a devotee of love doesn't care about any religion, today I declare you, my god. I have my temples in the crook of your body and, I place my holy offerings on your lips, neck, and jaw. I trace your soft skin with passion; Your name is deeply engraved on my soul.

- Rani Hirani

32. About the writer

About the writer:

Rani Hirani

Rani Hirani is a teen introvert writer, embracing her life in the pieces of poetry, books and solitude. Writing heals her and inspires her whenever she is having a cumbersome day. Apart from this, she is a BTech student, a content writing intern and runs a Spotify podcast, The Evenfall Stories.

33. A letter to my 15 year old self

Hey ,

You just got the opportunity of hosting the entire Christmas event of your school. Standing in front of the mirror all day and rehearsing your speech with that one broken comb which you have taken for a mic. you are excited coz now from being on the stage for short morning assemblies , you will be the face of the entire event . but ,how do I tell you? should I ?you need to know this, though . day 2 of rehearsal and you'll be sharing your part with one of your comrades . Hey, don't be crestfallen ,though . your expressions ,diction personality, and confidence ,will make the bishop of Meerut diocese so moved ,that, he , the big man of Meerut, will end up in the playground after searching for you so hard, just to tell you that, " you are the best speaker he has ever come ever come across. god bless you my child". and suddenly sharing your part with someone else won't seem to be an upsetting issue anymore. you will learn that quality matters than quantity and your journey of being an orator and writer will start from here .

just one thing you will be so busy in meeting the expectations of your principal ,teachers and yourself that you won't enjoy the achievements you will be bestowed with .so relax and live them. please .before it gets too late. live them. as you'll grow older, you will start losing friends and in this process you will start questioning your self worth . things like ,"am I not enough"? will start popping up .you will be crying yourself to sleep every night .

I am sorry that you have to go through this when you don't even deserve even half of it. but guess what after going through this you will come back stronger and you be able to distinguish between the real and fake ones. but just stop being too available for everyone every time . they'll start taking you for granted this way. Speak up . Voice out if you feel insulted or uncomfortable .stop feeling that they have a heart when they are hurting yours. you don't owe anyone anything. don't be hard on yourself. and it's ok if you luck in love wasn't good. You'll want to be all by yourself , staying in your room all day long and never wanting to come out of it . You'll start running away from people , emotions and feelings so much that you'll not even come to know that you've also started running away from yourself. Communicating will get hard . You'll be turning cold on the surface , but deep down , you'll be that kind and empathetic girl , who'll go the extra mile for anyone in need. try and trust yourself that you will attract good things and good people in life. don't box yourself from your past experiences. it is worse, trust me. you deserve all that you ever dreamt of and all that you don't even think you do .just stop feeling that you aren't enough. you are more than enough. your sister's can do, what you can't .I know .but, guess what? you can do, what they can't. they can't be *"Shubhangi*" the way you can be.So, cherish yourself. you are one and only one .let yourself breathe bloom. stop competing with your classmates and start competing with yourself. attain the highest level of perfection .explore everything and every field. reach out to your people when you feel low. ask for help. there's nothing wrong in that. but ,at the same time, learn how to be emotionally independent, and ,then you've got this. stop running a maddening rat race against time .forget about ,who will win or lose ,you will get mentally exhausted in this process, love. don't force things to happen, let things be. and give priority to your mental peace .and please stop pleasing everyone you will leave yourself way too behind in this. and yes, taking a break is not a big deal .mental health is important. and if something makes you happy to you then it doesn't have to make sense to anybody else. write a journal on a daily basis .keep track of your emotions. know yourself instead of trying hard to know temporary people in your life . A bit later , l puberty will hit you, and you will know what menstruation is. you will be told by neighbourhood aunties that hide it from boys .but,thanks to your wonderful mumma , that she taught you that , menstruation is natural and normal and not something to be ashamed of. it's nothing to be hidden .and I am proud of you that you questioned the shopkeeper that ,"why is he wrapping sanitary napkins in black polythene whereas he's wrapping The other stuffs in o white one "?break stereotypes.

you don't need to be conditioned. as time will pass by ,you will be told to sit like a" girl " . you'll get to listen , "why you so skinny"?" gain some weight"." apply under eye cream to your dark circles"." why don't you treat your pimples their growing with the same speed as the money plant in your garden"? but, hold on love. you don't need to fit in or sit , talk ,walk or look a certain way just to please others and make yourself uncomfortable. and yes ,you have the *most beautiful smile*, don't feel insecure about it. it's a magical one, trust me .and not to forget, please ,don't apply toothpaste on pimples. this don't work at all ,you idiot(laughs). moreover, continue using Johnson's baby, there's no shame in it .just be comfortable in your own skin .don't get boxed .*fly high but stay grounded*.mumma is a very good consultant .just stay by her side and love her a little more she is gone through a lot of shit .give papa a hug, for keeping you before himself every time his role gets overshadowed by he has been the best father you could ever have. remember ?how happy he was when he came from his office with a big smile on his face and told mumma that they would call you "Shubhangi "? And please no matter what the situation was ,they never failed to give you everything you needed and wanted .so don't let them starve for your five minutes in a day, when you will be in your twenties. you are important to them .just say," *I love you* " more often, this will be the biggest gift to them. papa just wants a secured future for you .so when he'll say, "pursue engineering". do it .say yes. I know it's boring but why not do it happily for that one man who loves you unconditionally and will never hurt you .one more thing you've got the best parents and brother and they deserve all the best things . dream and achieve all that you want and give them all what they long for and they and their sacrifices very well deserve,so that all of what they went through doesn't go in vain . Bear fruits to their labour . dream dream and dream don't stop writing please. this is you.

in the end , I've written a poem for you .don't judge, huh . I am better than you(laughs)

Stop compromising, start comprehending, be you ,

The water is wild and roaring, but, I know, you will sail through.

You look beautiful even with your small eyes, dark circles and those stubborn pimples,

All you need to do is, to confidently own them and smile a little.

Engineering is boring, I know ,but, how about writing constantly, playing guitar and dancing to your favourite tunes ?

believe in yourself, love yourself ,cry sometimes, it's okay , and with respect to boys? Darling, stay immune.

You are enough and pretty inside out,

And it doesn't matter ,if you don't know how to pout .

Don't let insta likes and comments validate who you are,

Coz, let me tell you that you're a gem of a person, yes , you truly are !

- Shubhangi Bhardwaj

34. Break me again

Break me again , please !

I am unable to write something good .

I need you to do a favour for me .

can you break me again ? please?

I am falling in love with this pain, this emptiness , this stillness, this pain is the one who's helping me out these days.

broken but wanna break myself again , this time , a lot more break me as deep as possible this won't hurt me anymore .

By breaking me, you're just make me a fine person

I want you to get close to me even closer I want you to become my habit in a way that if I don't talk to you for a day I start to feel a void come into my life and hug me tight say words those sweet little lies and then I would Sigh, scream, yell, cry ,for your love which you won't give me anymore.

Everything starts getting intense and then boom

you change

you start to dislike me

the things which made you laugh earlier now are the ones which make you irritated and then one day

you pack your stuff

and leave

and take my everything with you

my love

my care

my heart

my soft side

my emotions

my tears

my love

my something

my everything

and leave me behind with my nothing and pain

this would leave me totally broken every piece hither and thither and so far away from each other that reaching to one piece would seem getting distant from the other

even after hustling hard if I were to bring all the pieces together yet I would not be able to fix it cause they are broken so finely

I want to lose so that when I win I have a chest full of my learnings

I am tired of writing with my pen and words I wanna try writing with my tears

promise me love and then even forget our friendship

don't fake your good side show me your dark one

don't touch my heart just I aim at it and break it

stop giving excuses and say a blunt ,straight no

after being so into me , make me stand on the pedestal of High Hopes and then,

stop talking to me and don't even give me the reason .

let me run like a thirsty cat(thirsty here means thirst of the lost love) here and there in search of your love (water) till I'm exhausted

And then, one fine day, you see me searching for you with a hopeless face teary eyes ,I look at you , you look at me and you walk away .

set my hopes high but don't let me in fully . make sweet memories that I can never get enough of

Don't let me forget you

as soon as I am on the verge of forgetting you come back , apologize,

talk with those comforting lies make me happy make me smile and then leave again break me...break me inside out

I'll start writing more beautifully then ig ...

Coz when a broken heart writes nothing in the world can beat its beauty and fineness.

- Shubhangi Bhardwaj

35. Our if's and parents

If, at any point of time, you feel lonely. just remember, there is a woman in your life who waits for your "hi man a, I am doing good " call , every night before going to sleep .if, at any point of time ,you feel that you've nothing to brag about what you where you went last summer unlike your friends. just remember, your father wore the same old kurta on this Diwali because you wanted an iPhone as a Diwali gift. if, at any point of time , you feel like running away from your parents house because you feel restricted . just remember , that once you leave that house ,you'll long to go back to these two persons each night who were actually protecting you from any harm and danger . if, at any point of time, you feel like your parents are getting too much into your life and your friend circle . just remember, that every time they warned you against that one friend of yours , they were actually right . if ,at any point of time ,you feel like they are asking too much from you. just remember, what they did for you is not even half of it and you can't even repay it all your life .they have been and they still are going the extra mile just for you .some of it you know and some you don't . if seeing them getting aged day by day, you feel like they're getting way to kiddish. just remember, they used to hold you in their arms all day long and still never get bored of you .so ,with them getting older, be a little more patient, loving and caring .it's your time to parent them .say I love you more often and hug them without any reason.Make them feel wanted and special . Treat them the way they treated you when you were a kid . remember, they have gardened you well and now it's your turn to let them enjoy the fruits of their labour.

If you fail now , it will not be you , it'll be them who'll feel failed as a parent . Don't let them fail.

- Shubhangi Bhardwaj

36. About the writer

About the writer:

Shubhangi Bhardwaj

Shubhangi is an introvert sprinkler system . She has her
another world set up in the beauty of full moon, twinkling
stars, calm mountains and chasing sunsets. She is an avid
reader, budding writer, passionate dancer, soulful singer and
an engineering student. Longing to live, laugh and grow !

37. Dreaming

I want to cry.

I want to scream.

I want my mind to stop thinking

Cause I can't live like this anymore,

But I can do nothing but dreaming.

Dreaming of a better life that will maybe never happen;

Of the perfect love who could help me healing,

Of the life where I could achieve my own goals and not the one that other set for me.

But right now I'm just dreaming

And crying silently

And wearing this mask who make me look strong

Even if I'm the weakest inside.

- Marie

38. I am human

Why does it always finish the same way ?
Why is it always me who is crying
And you who doesn't care at all ?
I am not a doll with no feeling
A stone you can threw.
I am human
With feelings
With emotions
And I won't let you destroy me again.

- Marie

39. Keep hoping

Keep hoping in the future
Even in the darkness.
It is just a matter of days
For your life to change.
It is just a matter of people
For your mood to shift.

- Marie

40. She

Her heart was full of love
That got stolen by a world
Who used her then threw her.
She is love
But she is a human
Who can say no too.
She is hope
Who still believe in better days
While fighting her darkness.

- Marie

41. Butterflies

Human are like butterflies.

All different and unique.

Our flaws don't make us ugly.

Our imperfections make us beautiful.

Our only fault is that we don't know how to spread our wings

To fly

To fly higher and alone to our dreams and happiness.

- Marie

42. Diamond

I'm that song you skipped
And found out later it was fire.
I'm that kid you bullied
Thinking she was weaker.
I'm that girl you ignore
And realised she was the one.
You did the mistake to undervalue my worth.
Well I'm a diamond and if you can't see it
Then it's because you don't deserve me.
And even if I have to wait an eternity
Then I'll wait until the right one see my real worth
And treat me as a diamond.

- Marie

43. About the writer

<u>About the writer:</u>

Marie is a french woman of 23 years old. She is passionate about mental health, nutrition and all form of self-care. She started writing poetry to express all what she was keeping for herself; the good, the bad and her dreams, hoping her writings would inspire and heal people like it does with her.

44. Dandelion

O Dandelion , rich and proud
King of village flowers.
Every day is a Coronation day -
With that gleaming aura of yours

–

You have no triumphant hours
But are always the humble one ;
I like to see you smile
To beat the blue grass-spears

–

Your yellow heads are cut away
Yet to stand head held high
By noon you shine again
More golden than ever.

–

But as the raven spreads his wings
So dark and murky ,
Sucking up the merriment
The grim environment grows again.

–

The uninvited guest knocks on wood
As the boughs shake fearing ,
The still winds pen a tale

Of the gruesome presence.

–

O , dandelion , you kind soul,

Whisper of healing kisses,

And a warm heart wave your wand

From the grips of the grim , free the world.

- Debodreta Mazumder

45. To an online friend who is closer than my real life friend

Open letter to an online friend who is closer than my real life friend.

It was around this time , last year when I met this person. Just like a friendly , cheerful pup I was always eager to make friends but somehow got backstabbed by a handful of them. Brooding over the ongoing not-so-important problems of mine , I was talking to a new group of friends where I recently got added for a project. I felt warm, wanted and loved - I felt included for the very first time. I was blinded by all these emotions of mine when someone tapped on my door , chat box in this case. We had some similar interests and so we bonded well. Gradually I found an inspiring and motivating elder sister in her and she found a younger sister in me , of whom she could take care of. She taught me to stand up even after falling hard and bruising my knees , she patted my back when I brought an A+ in my board exams , she encouraged me to take up several challenges and opportunities in order to test myself. A simple T-H-A-N-K-Y-O-U or any other materialistic gift can never convey how much thankful or grateful I am. With her , I neither had to suffocate my happy wishes nor muffle my vulnerable tears. I can never thank her enough for showing me the stronger side of myself , ME.

- Debodreta Mazumder

46. Nightfall

He's the nightfall , so serene and fine
Stands graciously head held high
Beautiful and faint smile of him,
He is a beautiful sight.

–

Watches the butterfly slowly
And calmly flapping its wings;
Through the mists to the valley
Distant as it goes.

–

Embraced by the darkness shines so bright
He comes just like a mellow dream ;
So peaceful and soothing
Wiping away the teardrops of frightful hearts.

- Debodreta Mazumder

47. Just like you do

I look up to you everyday
So that I can stand upright
Just like you do
Carrying numerous loads on your back

–

I want to shine brighter
Just like you do
Shine even brighter
When there's a flame inside you

–

Like you, I want to find gold
So that I can burn
And carve my heart
Just like you do.

–

Just like you do
Remind us of not being only a noun
A pronoun , an adjective or an adverb
But a human myself.

–

You write your name like a logo
As no one owns you
Except you

I want to thank you for being you
Just like you do.
- Debodreta Mazumder

48. Waves

Like the waves
My words might brush up
Against your shore
Obscured by time

–

Every scribble faded
And so did the unsaid emotions
The blanched land
White waves crashing against those rocks
Wash away your presence

–

Don't leave me alone by the waves
They remind me of you
Unbound and carefree
Just like the bird
You fly
Beyond the horizon.
- Debodreta Mazumder

49. About the writer

About the writer:

Debodreta Mazumder

Debodreta , a 18 year old student loves scribbling her rough thoughts in the back of her notebook. With a pen and a bunch of papers , she's a bird ready to fly high , beyond the horizon.

50. The river called

Sitting at the edge of the bridge, looking at the beautiful sunset, the small waves forming in the river's water, looking oh so alive as if trying to cheer me up. The glistening water washes away the banks and all the fatigue out of me.

After work, I come here and just look at the river like this for hours. I don't miss a single day.
This place has been my favorite spot because she liked it.

She loved the peace and the sound of the river. It was so far away from our place but she used to come here every weekend and drag me with her too.

When I asked her why she likes to come here, she used to give me the most sincere smile and say, "Don't you like it too? When I come here, it feels like I am free from all the worldly chaos and responsibilities. It feels like it's calling me. It's beautiful out here and It's the only place that hasn't changed in the last 10 years."

"And me? I haven't changed too right?" I asked her with my expectant puppy eyes.
She burst into a laughter fit and gave me a slight bump on the

shoulder.

"No, you are still a loser!" She was still laughing.

I loved that part of her. I loved everything about her.

But I don't know why I can't help but hate her now.
This river was our place.
'OUR'
Not just hers.
How dare she take it for herself?

If only I was there, to listen to her. She was calling me.
But I didn't listen.
Then the river called.
And she picked up.
- Aaradhya Tiwari

51. Sakura and You

Dear Archie,

It's been a long time. I hope you remember me.
We never got the time to catch up so I thought of writing you this letter.

I am sitting near the sea shore, the water is washing away the sand on my feet and foaming up at places. The tides are low and calm.

I can see the little hermit crabs running after each other.
It's quiet, no one's around, just the voice of the sea echoing in my ears.

The sky is starting to get dark but not yet.
It's taking the color of beautiful cherry blossoms and turning crimson towards the horizon.

Spring is almost here. Sakura will be in full bloom. You remember the time we went for a walk among the cherry blossoms garden in Spring. It was so beautiful.

I can picture you smiling when you read this. Your smile took all my worries away.

I still have that picture with me. You were glowing, you still do.

I knew you were capable of great things, and it all came true. Congratulations on your new movie!

I wish I could be there with you but we both know that it wouldn't have worked out.

Don't beat yourself up about it, it was my decision, all from breaking up to moving away and this letter too.

I am taking my last decision today, Archie.

When you will get this letter, come find me underneath the Sakura tree.

I'll be there, resting in peace, waiting for you.

Goodbye.

Love
Lauren
- Aaradhya Tiwari

52. About the writer

About the writer:

Aaradhya Tiwari

Aaradhya is known for being the go-to person for everything. She enjoys reading tragic stories, yet she always strives to bring positive energy into the room. She enjoys writing as much as she enjoys Khaled Hosseini's work. Her regular companions are comics and food, and she enjoys delving into music occasionally. If you see her somewhere, she isn't angry or sad, it's just her face. Go ahead and say hi, you will be greeted with a warm smile and hugs (covid-free)

53. My Soul

If I had to define my soul into words,

It would be a nuisance for it to be identify as human.

For it wears faded lilac over a pale body,

Frantically hasty bandages on crafty feline sin,

Legs have scars covered in a sheet of white cotton strips with utter care,

And eyes tired and dull of cruelty and hardships.

Bloody cracks cover it's face.

For residing in a broken body,

Tortures it's fate.

Yet it stays, bound to it like puppet and strings.

Wondering if the body is the puppet,

Or has it been tied to those strings,

It crumbles into the pool of indigo sea.

The crack slowly seeping,

Rainbow of creativity.

- Ananyaa Sharma

54. Where the Darkness Resides

Where there is darkness.

There is an uncertainty of whether the devil resides or the unknown imagination of a senses bound human.

The darkness isn't the fear itself,

It's the human fear of being with something negative in that darkness.

For what the human doesn't know,

Is what if considers damned, condemned and negative to it's flexible soul.

- Ananyaa Sharma

55. Our Summer

Our summer were covered with burning hot climate and riots.
Our summer was deaths and masks on our faces.
Depression and online classes,
Hardships and internships,
Free time and friends, became a distant memory of the past.
Quarrels and bondings brew into the halls of a lonely home.
New hobbies and old passions,
Came alive as we grew into the walls of the home.
Our summer was a gruesome war of humanity and humans.
Yet hope resided for the unending future of the world caving.
- Ananyaa Sharma

56. About the writer

About the writer:

Ananyaa Sharma

Ananyaa (Haru) often can be seen listening to music and reading books on their laptop. They like doodling and can be found researching on random topics at any given moment. They believe that words have powers that are equivalent to magic in books.

57. Will you cry when I die

For some reason or other,
We have parted our ways.
You are not mine,
Anymore.
My misfortune, I know.
But I
Am yours and will remain so
Forever!

–

The fear of losing you
Has always been my worst nightmare.
But what about you?
Has the thought of my death,
Ever scared you?

–

What if,
All of a sudden,
One fine day,
You find me on the deathbed.
Will your heart scream,
Even just for a minute?
Will your garden
With an array of beautiful flowers,

Lose its lusture?

Will your eyelids droop?

And if it happens,

Will my image flash into your mind, in an instant?

Will the hand

Which I used to hold,

Fist out of heartbreak?

Will your days turn pale?

And at night,

Will my memories haunt you?

Will the smile on your face;

I used to fall for, every single time,

Fade away out of despondency?

Will the clink of the anklets, out of nowhere,

Remind you of me?

Will the photo of mine

Which you used to adore a lot,

Find a place in your wallet?

Will the drips of rain

Bring with it a flash of remembrance,

When we would dance and get drenched together?

–

But above all,

Apart from everything,

Will the drops of tear,

Roll down from your eyes?

Will you even cry,

When I die?

- Deepsikha Mohapatra

58. A Lover Like No Other

They say,
Opposites attract.
Nay!
Not every time.
Sometimes
Instead of the sparkle,
The shock is severe.
The thing
That keeps the arguement between us
Always fuelled,
Is
The Definition of Love!
You don't express anything,
And my naive heart
Can't hide anything.

—

I always have asked you,
"Don't you think
My texting and calling you
Hundred times
Before you reach home safe,
Is love?

My writing poems and long paragraphs
Only to make you feel
How special you are to me,
Is love?
Your falling ill
And my heart weeping;
Praying for your quick recovery,
Is love?
That wide smile on my face
And I stepping the La-La Land
Whenever I receive a message from you,
Is love?
With the mere excuse of books
My going to you
And your waiting for me on the balcony,
Is love?
Your giving me chocolates inside a book
And my eating up on the roof
Without showing and sharing,
Is love?
Our sudden unexpected meets;
Out of nowhere
And my heart skipping a bit,
Is love?"
And my list goes on and on.

–

But,

You keep on saying,
"Let my definition
Remain
Unsaid,
Unexpressed,
Unvoiced."

–

I realised this,
So very late.
If the love is strong
Nothing can separate us.
In the midst of the shocks,
We still can find
That bright sparkle.

–

My conveying my feelings before the whole world;
Your keeping it just upto yourself,
Why don't we think
The river that flows
Between the two contrasting banks
Keeping it connected,
Forever,
Is love?
- Deepsikha Mohapatra

59. Beauty lies within

In the world of perfection, I prefer your flaws.
In the world of luminance, I prefer your being blind and grey.
In the world of rose petals, I prefer your thorns.
For I have read your book
While others judged you just by the cover.
And yes, whenever you feel lonely,
Be assured, you are not.
Since another broken heart is forever there
With you;
Trying to mend yours
Which seems like a jigsaw puzzle.
Me, failing many times,
To arrange
And rearrange
But never feeling failed;
For my realm of despair
May not be the same as yours;
However, my infuriation is somewhat;
Beyond the horizon,
Deeper than the ocean.

—

So and such is the human character,I believe
To stain others,

To slap others.
To err is human
But to lambaste, incessantly, is an act of sheer inhumanity.
And that is what people do;
Without any shame.

–

Anytime I have asked, " How are you?"
Your quick reply has been, "I am very fine," with a cheerful
face and no tint of ache.
But deep down inside, I know
You are not the real you.
Those endless tortures have scratched your soul;
Those unending barrage of taunts have demoralised you;
Thus, the dismal consequences have voided you.

–

I fear of your doing someting fatal,
Out of exasperation.
But before taking any such step
My dear friend, keep in mind,
The Moon is loved,
In all its forms,
In all its phases,
Along with the scars it possesses.
Everyone is uniquely beautiful;
And have their own tales to tell,
Their own anecdotes to express.

–

So each time you are full of,

The pent up emotions and frustrations,

Just vent it.

Because,

You are beautiful in your own way.

Very beautiful, indeed!

So, I say

The surface is only seen,

While the beauty lies within.

- Deepsikha Mohapatra

60. About the writer

About the writer:

Deepsikha Mohapatra

Pursuing a bachelor's degree in Political Science, the author, Deepsikha Mohapatra questions the hurtful yet important aspects of life with a touch of vintage background. Somewhere in the easy going mature lady, there is a child hidden in her always curious about everything going around. She sees the world as an opportunity yet gets pulled back by the laws and norms therefore penning down her every feeling.

61. Khuli Kitaab

Bikhre hue Hain panne khuli kitaab ke,

Rakhna tumhe hai unko ab Zara sambhaal ke

Har modd par khadi hai,

Chhuke bhi anchhui hai,

Yeh naaz Kar rhi hai Apne sawaal pe...

Rakhna unhe hai tumko ab Zara sambhaal ke,

Bikhre hue Hain panne khuli kitaab ke.

- Ananya Mani

62. Sach hai ya Nahi

Sach Nahi hai Yaha Kuch bhi,

Sab jhoot ke saaye hain.

Poochte Hain yeh phir bhi humse,

Ki Apne Hain ya paraaye hain.

Jaanke Accha Lagta hai ki door hi Sahi par paas hain...

Mere toh Kuch bhi nhi yeh,

Par auron ke khaas Hain..

Mere toh Kuch bhi nhi yeh,

Par auron ke khaas Hain.

- Ananya Mani

63. An Open letter to Phoebe Buffay

Dear Phoebe,

Or shall I say Princess Consuella Banana Hammock?

When I first met you I knew you are different from your friends. Gradually I came to know why. When I look back to your childhood...well it was not a bed of roses. To lose your mother and live on the street at an young age when most of the kids around you would go to school and had a perfect family to grow up, well it's pretty hard. Only someone who has suffered a fate like you would feel your pain. The extraordinary part about you is despite the hardships your faced, you turned out to be a hell of sunshine. Thinking about you brings a smile on my face and all my sadness departs. You are the most loving friend a person could ever ask for. And boy nobody would try to hurt animals Infront of you...or it's an end game for them. You believe in moving on.. However hard the past could have been. You gave the biggest sacrifice of your life for your half brother and didn't even think on it while deciding to do so. For you it wasn't a sacrifice..but the greatest gift of happiness you could ever give to anyone. You treated your father and biological mother with a kind heart. You knew your life would be different and far more easy if they hadn't forsaken you...How do you have such a big heart?

Do people like you still exist in this world? Kindness is just a fraction of your personality Miss Regina Fellange,

but you are quirky too and talented as hell. You immortalised all the smelly cats in the world. They owe it to you girl!

Closing my letter to you with the lingering thoughts of your wedding night. You got your Crap Bag to keep you happy forever. You deserved it girl…you deserved it!

Yours truly,
Ananya Mani

64. About the writer

About the writer:

Ananya Mani

Ambivert by nature, her heart yearns for writing, art, plants,
a ginger tea and a nice company to share all these with.
Writing reviews, watching movies and series and simply
chilling with her friends, family and own self forms pretty
much her life.

65. Dear heart, you know it all

I visit them on the days I don't feel myself. They keep me alive. Or maybe not.

One doesn't even know that he lives in my heart, I never told him. If I had, he would've walked out of it just like he did of my life. I told him he had my heart so he returned it while going away , I couldn't risk his life in my heart .

My heart is half a breath away from hurting and healing. I need to save my heart at all costs , it has kept all the lives alive which are actually not.

One ended itself while finding answers to life, he lives in my heart , stays in a corner , silent , as if mourning to his own death.

The life of my younger self lives here too, she doesn't want to die and always questions why I want to kill her.

The life of my dreams occupies a huge space of my heart, doesn't let the others enter my heart. It seems the society doesn't let her live and now as a revenge, she doesn't let the others in.

One is my own self , doesn't wants be out there in the world, says no one will truly understand her , so I keep her safe in my heart, forever.

TO THE LIVES IN MY HEART,
PLEASE DON'T DIE.

- Priyanka Suthar

66. A list of things I want you to do for me after I'm gone

1. Don't cry , I know it's ironic. I don't want anyone to remember me as someone who cried a lot , I'm a lot more and a lot less than that.

2. Continue visiting that old lady by the street who laughed at our dumb and lame jokes. You'll find me in the genuine smile of hers.

3. Watch the sunset twice, read that book twice, call that lady beautiful twice, listen to our favourite song twice, pet that dog twice, ONCE FOR YOU, ONCE FOR ME.

4. Walk and dance a little longer on the favourite footpath of ours, if a flower falls down don't forget to pick it up and give it to a stranger like we always do.

5. Don't let my name die, chant like it's keeping you alive.

6. You always asked me why I listened to songs at such low volume, you also do it. I keep it low because I want people's voice to be audible whenever they call out for help or for nothing. You know how much I love helping others.

7. Try loving yourself like I did , do and will forever do. It's tough , I know. Try your best though.

8. Continue messing the kitchen and missing me because now you won't find anyone to laugh at that stupid laugh of yours.

What's the best way to keep a dead person alive other than feeling things for them? Never stop feeling.

P.S : keep sharing memes , I might need them when I cry or miss you.

- Priyanka Suthar

67. To the deleted selfie

To the deleted selfie,
It wasn't your fault, really. We tend to get rid of the things which didn't turn out as our expectations. In that one selfie , I was grinning, alot. I thought people would look at my teeth and call them imperfect.

There is nothing I can do except bury my love for you. People have raised the standards so high that my height won't reach it , no matter how hard I try to jump, higher each time.

Insecurities knocked and said "To say I LOVE YOU , one must know first how to say I" and made a leave. I is just an alphabet when it belongs to me, but when I've to talk as a first person, I don't know why something starting with I ends with you. It's never I love myself and always I love you.

Confidence is somewhere lost between midnight fears and tears. Amidst which confidence loses its energy and Insecurities are somehow louder, always. I now know why something like recycle bin exists, to give life to something which we tried to end, believing the standards raised by someone else are for us too. Except that they're not, we have our own standards for our own height.

You said I killed you , haunt me then.

Tumhe agar mujhme aur tujhme chunne ka mauka mile toh,
Tum khud ko hi chunna

- Priyanka Suthar

68. Him and Hope

People come and go, the cycle keeps repeating. Can it stop for once , atleast when it was you who had to stay. Change is constant and that's the biggest irony of my life. When I go home carrying the world's weight on my head to find some peace it reminds me of you, says I'm not myself without you. It's taking revenge of my past, I'd tell my home that I don't feel at home without him and now home refuses to even recognise me without him.

Him and home were never different, I atleast believed I'd never find a need to seperate them. I loved coming home with him. Now I realise it was him who made my home actually home. My home betrays and asks for him in a way screaming "I'm not your home, your calling wrong house your home, it's him, it was always him". I have hopes of you returning, if not for me, atleast to make this house - home. My home misses you more than I miss home, you. Come back to home, will you?

While I was understanding home and him are the same, you tried your best to prove me wrong and I failed at it miserably. You remind me of me and my home that it's home and not just a four walled house.

Dear hope ,

Don't ever lose hopes on me, I'm trying my best.

POV - Him is a person called hope

- Priyanka Suthar

69. To the boy who reminds me of me

Pour rain over my rotten body, like you always did. You won't do it anymore, will you? You won't be here, I won't be here. Our words will remain, they'll get repeated everytime someone falls in love, to express thier love using the words we express our love.

Your name has more meaning about love than the word "love" will ever have.
It's tough to write about something you haven't experienced at all. A bit easier if you've imagined the scenarios in your heart a million times or maybe a little more or less. Love, for me is something like that.

I always mess up first things, the first Iloveyou was said to someone who didn't have a clue about my existence. What if I mess up love too? What if I mess up being in love with the person I love being myself the most? What if I mess up us? I don't think we are a happy tomorrow anymore, you and me.

I look at the box which is placed at a corner, or thrown away there. I search love in it, love in the torn photograph and the torn love letters. You can get rid of the love letters but you can't get rid of the love, can you? The love between the spaces of each word you wrote for me, about me? The love I can see in the photograph, your smile is still the same. Like I always told, reality with some fiction. Your smile feels so real and bright, it takes me to magical places, I didn't even know existed. Hence, reality with some fiction sprinkled.

Your memories have created a town in my heart which I can't help but visit each time I hear the word love, or any word. Everything reminds me of you. Can you stop it? Stop *a long pause* loving me. There, I said it.

From,
Someone, who is still a fan of your smile.

- Priyanka Suthar

70. Yeh khula aasman, aagaye hum kahan

I like to believe that clouds move a bit slower when I'm looking at them. In a way trying to say "We're here". But only for a while. And when they form beautiful shapes, trying to say "You're going to be okay"

I like the sun but sometimes it's too much to handle. The clouds cover it in a way to say "We got your back, mate"

I wonder if there is a way to say to them that it is okay to feel heavy sometimes. That it is okay to let it out if it gets a lot inside. That their tears are the second most beautiful ones I've ever seen. First, always remains his.

Dear clouds,
It's okay to just vanish sometimes. We understand. We can appreciate clear skies somedays. We miss you tho, just saying. This is just a small token of my heart that I'm giving you for being there for me. All the times I thought I'll die out of period cramps, miserable feeling of not being loved, not loving enough, not being there for people, them not being

there for me and everything I've felt and all the things you know already. Thanks for being there, beside or above me. And tolerating my emotional dramas.

From,
Someone, who has half of her gallery filled with your pictures.
XOXO

- Priyanka Suthar

71. On holding on to your younger self

Holding something delicate as her, my hand started to shiver. Almost as if to say "You have no rights to". Her lips moved, she whispered to make sure it was audible to me and only me. It was loud enough to me tho, loud enough to hurt me in my heart ; listening to that voice and what she had said, "Don't hold me, the last time you did you almost ended me". I'm not sure about that. I try saying to her that if I can start loving her she can too. She hardly seems convinced. I try to say better or atleast the right words and later add that life will one day happen and find her and that she'll fall in love with life as I did. More, everyday. I'm sure about that , afterall she's me and I'm her. I know her and I want her to know me too. That I survived everything she thinks she can't. I made it through the tunnel and saw the bright side of it. I want her to be happy for me like I'm for her. I want her to know that the things she's worrying about, no one cares once you're 19 or strong enough to accept them yourself. I want to say so much to her, all the things I'm proud of, happy for and love. Everything and anything. She can just sit there and wonder how I made it through with so much confidence. She can stare at me in awe when I tell her about my beautiful life and get irritated when I tell her about the dumb stuff I still do. She can just be here.

I wish I could say all this to her. I wish you knew me like I know you. I wish we knew who saved whom. Or it was us in a whole. I wish.

We save the love in a photograph. We try to keep everything alive in the photograph. Even the dead. Especially our younger selves.

- Priyanka Suthar

72. About the writer

About the writer:

Priyanka Suthar

Priyanka is someone who believes being kind and long walks are the only ways to get through life. She has been a reader for as long as she can remember. For her, words combine to form a different world. She belongs to that world. She loves sky, pretty houses, deep conversations and everything else she can call home. Sometimes people too. Emphasis on sometimes.

73. A Familiar Stranger

I wonder who this man is, a boy who just left his home to
achieve his dreams or a middle-aged man whose
city and dreams both were sucked out of him?
Why is he standing here in this window, to jump off from it
and praying not to meet himself again in his
next life or to jump his wounded emotions off from his caked
and cracked chest?
What is he thinking, is he thinking about that friend who left
without a goodbye or that stranger's first
'Hi', who just hugged him in the first meeting crushing the
mortuary of his pain giving a hope to believe in
'forevers' again?
What is he looking at is he having good memories about that
crush who made the butterflies of his stomach
dance with just a little glimpse of her in the corridor or that
last hug of that partner who left saying they had
no future together taking the breath of that last butterfly away
in some void?
Is he missing someone who has come and already left breaking
the statue of his existence into pieces or
waiting for someone to come and hold him and join the
pieces of his identity, again?
Is he tired of eating alone or is he worrying about earning a

meal tomorrow?

Has he lost himself in that crowded home or found himself in the exclusion of his insecurities? Is he

asking the moon to give him some chills to dry his tears off before anyone looks at him or is he asking

for some warmth from himself to melt his hard and fake image which he built to please the world which

doesn't even belong to him?

Is he about to cry or has wiped his tears off after exhausting every bit of pain forever to feel the freshness

of the old rays of sun shining his new hopes? I wonder who this man is, a stranger?

Me? or

you?

- Nidhi Dixit

74. The cracked Vase

There is a theory that Billions and billions of years ago a giant celestial fireball collided with the Earth and
severed a little of its portion from it, forever. Although it never got back to the earth to fill its void, it
couldn't, but it turned itself into what we call our Moon today, and since then it is loving its part from the
distance. Maybe these tides, high or low, are the hiccups earth got when moon misses it sometimes a little
more, sometimes a little less and a no-tide day is still unheard of. Maybe it's not some effective centripetal
or fugal force, maybe it's just earth's heartaches and craving for moon which makes it let the moon pull it
towards it just to get a little closer to it and stole some moments of this hard-earned closeness from the
universe. They say the Earth never saw the other side of the moon, the far side, maybe because the moon
never wanted the earth to see its back, maybe because the mere thought of a bit more distant from earth
made it miserable.
The same theory pronounces that the void got filled and REPLACED, by water, like it bandaged the earth
by making itself calm and so the earth and loved it in its new own way. The word REPLACED here is

worth my doubt, because you know, the tides lift that water
only, and maybe it's not water but the blood
which spilled out when both were getting severed bit by bit.
Maybe it's the souvenir of their love, the last
sign of their togetherness as well as separation, maybe.

- Nidhi Dixit

75. A help from you to yourself

Ever noticed that beam of light entering, from the surface where the door leaves the earth in a

completely dark room devoid of even a single sigh of any photon?

Imagine yourself sitting in that room. You cannot see even your existence in that darkness

neither of the room's. And then on a fine day a beam of light intrudes, it doesn't lighten up the

room to make you see anything much of yours or of room, but it makes you aware of the

presence of light on the other side. It makes you feel your blackened but still existing

existence when you come in its vicinity.

It answers all your 'whys' you have hammered before your 'reasons to exist'. It strikes you

benevolently to stir your cremated hopes. Although this change is not soothing or pleasant to

you, indeed you were suffocating in that darkness but you got used to it and honestly, hardly

prayed for such beam to enter, so when it stroked, you started feeling homesick. But this

smell of photons and the sight of the Brownian motion of the caked dust particles in that

room played a weird song in your inner self, familiarly unknown, although you are not really

liking it but simultaneously you are not even showing any strong desire to pause it. Is it just

some curiosity or an urge to crawl on to something new, that is your secret, unknown to you.

That room is your life, that scattered darkness is your negativity, and that beam is your own

hand towards yourself, resonating on a different frequency which you call your future.

That's You, rescuing yourself, making yourself aware of the existence of your ignorance,

taking yourself out of the cave to see the light acting as Socrates.

You are your own Socrates.

- Nidhi Dixit

76. Stormy Silence

I want to write Silence.

The strings of words which never got vomit out and left undigested those which ventured to the throat

where they were refused, painstakingly, to thrust out to assuage the rivalry heart beats. Heart takes it all,

those chambers suck in the emotions and throw them out. You see, the oxygenated emotions which you

tethered and mixed with your saliva and never let them rout out, they permeated down in there, getting

sucked in and kicked out in that same pattern, like that fly which just saw the last escape route shutting

down, it's trapped in travelling this journey, the same journey obnoxiously. Yes, it's Vapid, but wait,

whom are you blaming? You were the master of that ship, you harboured it in between the ocean. It will

sink one day with a storm, in Silence, a stormy silence.

And, I want to write that Silence.

- Nidhi Dixit

77. Void

I feel a void, inside me, i can feel it absolutely in the exact way a starving child feel in her stomach in the middle of a dark night. I can feel that in my whole body, like every cell of my body has been sucked out by this voidness. Every time i try to think, i feel like the nerves running to my brain got puntured in to get the thoughts out in the exact way my veins were punctured last week by the pathologist to know if my body is doing fine. I try, i try and try harder to think,to feel, to imagine, but there is nothing with which i can come up, absolutely nothing, i feel numb in the exact way the protagonist of that story in my class 10th literature book described, while he was drowning in that huge pool. They puntured my veins to know what is wrong with me, i mourn in pain with a hope, (un) fortunately they found nothing more than another virus , solutions for which injected more bitterness inside me for this world in the exact way the needles barged into the only thing living inside me. Now there is something inside me more than just a void, darkness, bitterness, for every single thing existing around me which i used to love or maybe just used to like, to make a difference between the two was always hard for me but it's even harder now, in the exact way it is to love, again, for that widow of a child marriage.

I feel more than a void inside me, i feel smothering my ownself in the exact way a victim of rape feels while standing in the Court of SOCIETY.

I crave for peace, i crave for me.

78. About the Writer

About the Writer :

Nidhi Dixit

Nidhi is a law student, an amateur writer, an editor, a speaker and an avid reader, all by choice tracking her way to positivity through the fog of negativity. She loves her own company. Her love for independence and liberal thoughts is inevitable. Books are her escape route to peace. Doodling and Mandala Art make her a beginner. Her ability to talk on every topic will impress you and her deep conversations work as calmness to hurrying hearts.

79. An immortal life

[Twenty Rules to become Immortal]

–

Mould yourself with such integrity
Adorn your speech with truth
Enrich your heart with generosity
And present yourself with dignity and couth.

–

No virtue is as precious as discipline
No habit is better than keeping oneself clean
No mind can become sharp without good listening skill
None, but patience and perseverance would make you determined and tranquil.

–

No matter how heavy the baggage of morals gets,
Notwithstanding the journey of life be long and vast,
In order to live a life free of regrets,
You must, travel with vim and zest till the last.

–

Always control your anger;keep your intentions pure
Conquer your fears;overcome your ephemeral lure.
The wisest you can grow is by valuing your time,
While pursuing these personality traits would surely make you sublime.

—

Besides all, you should consistently work as if
Fortune alone can't help you achieve your goal,
Simultaneously, pray to God with an utmost belief,
That only the Divine blessing can immortalise your soul.
-Naima Ansari

80. The echo within you

Forget the world, the philosophers and the mentors
Look deep into yourself and fetch out what stirs
That petty belief that makes you feel insignificant
Would damage your intellect, making you diffident.

–

Be by yourself, peacefully dwelling inside your heart,
Thinking, planning, hustling against the odds
Mark you! That's your real art.
Speak less, listen more - it makes you wise
Stay firm and adamant in your ways, even if they despise.

–

Let no fellow mate's success cause you self-doubt
Lest it should take away your will to bloom and sprout.
Life begs you, compels you or moans at you,
"Don't ever close your eyes, Take an overview. "

–

Grow big and sturdy with wisdom and confidence
Life ought not be hollow;I pray, "Green it deep and dense. "
Let not 'a farce melancholy', 'a gusty fear' or 'a capricious love'
Plunge out the power and vigilance from a flying dove.
-Naima Ansari

81. Homemaker: The Flightless Dove

I often wonder with distress
What compels the women of knowledge, strength and prowess
to give up their passion or ambition
Do you have an answer or can you even guess,
What subjects them into such submission?

—

Alas! I admire them with awe as well as pity
All those wives and mothers with dignity
Who have the power to achieve everything through their will
If they honestly dedicate themselves to their skill.
Even those maidens who seem hard to tame
Subject themselves to their spouse or children at the cost of their aim.

—

The kinds of women I've mentioned above
Oh! I have seen such 'flightless dove'.
How badly I wanna engage them all in a verbal fight
To ask if they got distracted or intentionally killed their might.
These unbeatable warriors ultimately accept their defeat
Perhaps thinking, "One man's poison is another man's meat. "

Are they sacrificing dreams in search for love and mirth?
Okay, but why at the risk of their self-worth?

—

To the dame reading this with a heavy heart
What makes it so difficult for you to restart?
To work on your goals bit by bit
Believe me! You definitely can achieve it through wisdom and wit
Don't let your dreams die for temporary joys, hey!
Don't waste your time gossiping, rather 'Seize the Day'!
To be expressive about your wants you need not be too loud
You can convince them just by whispering your heart out.
Stop existing only to please others, I beseech you!
Always have God in mind then choose what you want to pursue.
-Naima Ansari

82. The Naked Truth Of Lie

Would you be honest and tell me why
Is it better to die with a truth than to live with a lie?
To qualify for a good liar, you must possess some wit,
While the greatest benefit of truth is-you need not remember it.

–

If life were a plant, lie forms its shoots,
Growing deep inside the soil, truth forms its roots.

–

In the concert of life, lie is the melody in a song
While truth comes from the beat that's played all along.

–

Uttering truth is difficult, lying much easier
The voice of lie is feeble, truth more loud and clear.

–

Lie tastes sweet, truth quite bitter
True is a champion; a liar's a quitter.

–

Lie is the scum on the pond, truth - the water underneath
Truth is a swordsman's sharpest sabre; lie-its lustrous sheath.

–

Lie is abundantly lying everywhere
Truth is a treasure: rich and rare.

–

Lie is the wolf in a sheep's skin
Lie often comes hiding behind a grin.

–

Lie spreads hate, war, tremor and turmoil
Truth is the fate of innocents, harmoniously buried into the soil.

–

A chain of lies follows one to cover the bloodstain
A single strand of truth alone can move a big mountain.

–

Truth is like love and lust symbolise lie
Truth is the solemn reality one can never defy.

–

That the ugly truth of lie, lays naked before you,
Would you still quote saccharine lies, or rather be true?
-Naima Ansari

83. My Father: A Bliss To Me

Aren't you all waiting for me to brazenly unveil
My evergreen, pure and secret love tale?
I've woven it with great descriptive words, but to no avail
No matter how old it gets, this love would never go stale.

–

The chivalrous man, the hero of my dreams
Oh! His smile is brighter than the sunbeams.
He has been nourishing my thoughts since I were a little girl
Permeating my heart with immaculacy, to make it glisten like
a pearl.

–

He- the Guardian Angel has been protecting me from my
disguised foes,
Rectifying all my blunders with just words and no blows,
Constantly appreciating me in my highs, believing in me in
my lows,
Loving me with all my flaws, just as an anthophile loves a rose,
He has been all ears to my heart's silent echoes,
Oh! He is the supreme of all the superheroes.

–

Oft, he's gone against his will to execute my petty wants,
Patiently listened to all my ugly, stupid rants,

I've found bliss in his words, the kind of peace a young girl
would find in a man's arms,
Through him, I got closer to the Lord, abstaining myself from
the devil's charms.

–

Oh! My most empathetic man, a paragon of virtue,
What a blessing it is to have a Father as good as you, Abbu!
-Naima Ansari

84. About the writer

About the writer:

Naima Ansari

An eagle-eyed, budding fashion designer, and a poet aiming to be the 'She Wordsworth'.

85. To loose a beloved

The flowers weep
For the fallen willow tree
They knew what it was like
To loose a beloved
A friend from old times
A seeker of old laughs
The mourning flowers wilted
The petals fell
For they knew what it was like
To loose a beloved
A pretty smile
A kind and warm heart
The soil swallowed
The faded flowers
For it knew what it was like
To loose a beloved
A teary eyed goodbye
A broken but mending heart.
- Sania Baig

86. Waning Light

The bracelet of your words
Slashes my wrists
Yes it is your fault
But you're not the sole reason
Why I'm doing this

—

These people breathe
To steal away my mirth
But do they know
I am in no way
Lesser than what they're worth

—

I know that this too shall pass
Because nothing ever lasts
Not even my sorrows
To my delight
Because I thrive even in waning light.

- Sania Baig

87. Dandelions

The dandelions fly away
Carrying stories of lost hope and faith
Captivating eyes follow them
But they only lead us astray

–

I run behind them
I weep when I loose them
A brittle heart's wish broken
Hearing words that were never spoken

–

I see some dandelions descend
Burdened with so much hope
The wind couldn't carry them
There are some wounds that can't mend.

- Sania Baig

88. The Ghost

I'm a ghost
Destined to walk alone
These people, they mock me
They call me weak and drop me
These walls, they talk to me
They say what they have heard
Hence becoming my only helper

–

I'm a ghost
Destined to walk alone
These night lights, they blind me
And yet I can see
A plethora of your emotions
Strong but overwhelmed
Not weak, just a little disheartened

–

I'm a ghost
Destined to walk alone
I'm a shadow in the dark
Following you around
Until you loose your spark
I make you sit alone
And make you notice your flaws

Until you weep and ignore your perfection

—

I'm a ghost

Destined to walk alone

Nobody sees me slithering

Nobody notices me silently winning.

I win whenever you question yourself

I'm the reason you've lost faith

But worry not, my dearest

For I loose every time you utter

A word of forgiveness

- Sania Baig

89. Moving

It was a cold night,
The drizzle pittering and pattering down the window
I sat down with a cup of coffee in my hand,
Wondering when was the last time
I felt this peaceful at night.

–

A cold breeze swooshed,
Making the papers fly.
I looked at them and wondered
Why do I even write?

–

As I searched for answers within me,
Lost deep in thought,
Letting the bottle burst,
Tears sprang and flowed.

–

My grandma once told me years ago,
Letting talent go to waste is like
Acting paralysed when you can move.
"I'm moving, grandma" I whispered to myself.
- Sania Baig

90. About the writer

About the writer:

Sania Baig

Sania Baig is a young visionary who writes in an attempt to capture a part of her essence and portray it in front of the world. You'll often find her petting stray dogs, reading or daydreaming.

91. Tell Me This is Real and We Are Forever

Look into my eyes and tell me this is real, that we are Forever
;
Sing me a blue melody and make me yours.

Light me a stale cigarette and dance with me in the moonlight.

Paint my sorrows pink and draw bright yellow sunflowers on my thighs.

Put fallen flowers in my hair, and wrap me up in my Mother's favorite gown.

Let's lay down next to each other on a cold night and talk about everything we're afraid of. Let me lay down on your chest and listen to the rhythm of your heart and fall asleep in your arms.

I will dream of green meadows and running amongst a flock of sheep,

And when I wake up I wanna feel your breath against my skin and your arms tightly wrapped around me, afraid of letting me go.

And when you wake up, look into my eyes, give me a sleepy kiss and tell me this is real and we are forever.

- Devika P

92. A Letter to my 15-year-old self

Hey you,

This is your 20-year-old self, writing to you sitting on the same blue table you wrote: "You're going to get through this" with white glitter pen. I've made a few changes to our room (the walls are lavender now).

Are you crying on the bedroom floor again? Are you thinking of running away from home?

Are you looking at yourself in the mirror wondering that if you lose a little weight you'll look beautiful?

–

Darling, I'm so sorry that you have to go through this yourself. I wish I could show you how beautiful, strong and wonderful you are. You have nothing to worry about. You will grow up to be a strong independent, and a happy woman.

Don't hang on to him, he is not worth it. You're much more than that. He's going to play you over and over again. He's going to break your heart into a million pieces. You might feel as if you're never going to feel the same way about another guy. But that's nonsense, believe me.

–

Toothpaste doesn't help with pimples. Please stop using that. Try new hairstyles. Wear colorful clothes, stop wearing black.

Wear anything and everything you want. Your arms are not fat, please wear the white sleeveless dress to that wedding.

–

Keep reading those books that make you happy. Keep singing wonderful songs for Mom. Smile more. Eat more. Please don't starve yourself to fit into those jeans. Run around. Join the football team. Don't stay up too late fixing other's problems. Put yourself first.

–

If you feel alone and depressed, talk to Mom. She worries about us too much. I know she can be very nosy and a little over-protective at times, but she's also figuring it out, give her a chance.

Go give Dad a hug. He can't stand the fact that you're fifteen already. And he knows you're going to do well in your final exam.

Hey, I am writing this especially because I know how alone you feel right now. Highschool can be depressing. I know you're struggling. I know you cry yourself to sleep everyday I know you just want to stay in your bedroom and never come out. But it's going to get better. I need you to know that you're way more than High school dramas and heartbreaks. You deserve love like any other human being in this planet. I promise you; you are important.

–

Keep writing and keep believing in yourself. Explore things that give you happiness. Follow your dreams. Get up and try again and above all make mistakes.

I am so so proud of you. I love you.

Yours lovingly,

Devika

93. Paathu

It was a cold day of January 2018. I came home after a long day of school and tuitions. As soon as I reached home, my mom told me there was a small kitten under our car. Her leg was broken and she was limping. My mom had given her milk and biscuits. I told Mom as long as it stays outside the house, I'm fine with it. I thought it would go away once it's leg was healed.

A week passed, I was getting ready to go to school and this cat just walks inside the house as if it's her own, I ran upstairs because I was kind of scared of it. This became an everyday routine for the cat. She would stay downstairs behind the wall of the staircase and when I came down, she would pounce on me and I would race back upstairs. I think she loved it, because I swear I saw her smile wickedly.

Days passed, my mom named her Pathumma and we called her Paathu. My mom and my sister took care of her. My Dad and Paathu read the morning headlines together. My friends would come home just to play with Paathu. I didn't understand what the big deal was. I wouldn't go near her. It felt as if I had a new sister. Everyone gave her attention!

One day, I came home after a bad day at school and I was sitting in the veranda, when Paathu came and sat beside me, I was about to go inside because I thought as usual she was going to annoy me. But this time, she didn't do anything; it was as if she knew I had a bad day. She just sat near my leg. This became a daily routine, where we would share comfortable silences.

Slowly I started patting her and rubbing her back. She would eat ice-cream off my hands. I started telling Paathu almost everything. It felt like she understood me. And she would judge me EVERY single time. When I crack my lame jokes, she would either walk away or roll her eyes at me.

Paathu and I cuddled during rainy days, she would sit beside me when I studied, we watched TV together and we also have some neighborhood investigations together. I took care of her when she came home with random bruises. I would ask "Where do you run off to?" , she would give me a sly smile. We were the best of friends. Soon Paathu had kids and there were more cats in the house.

A year passed and I was off to college. I remember how Paathu was rubbing against my leg the whole day when she knew I wasn't going to be home everyday. I visited home during Vacations and Paathu would slowly come sit beside me because she didn't want to show too much affection (yes the big cat ego!).

Two months passed, I was in college, my mom called me and told me that most of our cats were dying because of a certain flu. I asked about Paathu and she said Paathu hadn't come home for days. I had this instant pain in my heart. It felt like my heart had broken into a million pieces. I cried and cried.

I told myself she was bored at home and she went on a big adventure because her best friend was thousand miles away from her.

Whenever I come home from college, it always feels like something is missing. Like our family isn't complete. Home was different without Paathu. But I still believe she's out there living her wildest dreams and once she's bored, she'll come home running to tell me all about it.

- Devika P

94. What if's of an overthinker

What if the dreams we've built up are just going to be a stagnant , abandoned fantasy only to be crumbled like the Lego house we made as a child?

What if the hope that we hold on to every night, is only going to be a mirage, never to be manifested? What if our whole life is just a twisted hallucination of a hopeless, desperate person , craving for satisfaction ? And what if, Happy Endings are an illusion and this is all we get ?

- Devika P

95. About the writer

About the writer:

Devika P

Devika is a final year bsc chemistry student. She's passionate about life and loves to write, sing and learn new things. She tries to find things that sets her soul on fire and she's hoping she'll achieve all her dreams one day

96. So close and yet so far

I am so in love with you. I don't know why and believe me; I am trying to figure out. Because everywhere I look, I see couples happy, mostly carefree and some serious enough to keep it under covers. I see faces laughing with happiness barely containable, leaking out like an overfilled bottle, lighting up the whole place. I am jealous, to be honest. Every relationship I've been a part of has ended quite prematurely, without solid reasons or a big ugly fight. Just two people falling out of love, not interested in the same things that they were looking for in the beginning.

Every girl was better than the previous one, so loving and cheerful. I've always questioned myself why I couldn't bring myself to love them like they loved me, like I love you. I've felt like I'm living a lie for all these years, and now my worst fears are coming true. Ever since I felt different emotions towards different people, which wasn't what was expected of me, I've been afraid of standing out of the crowd. And that has shaped my whole behavior. Always looking to blend in, never the first for anything, living my own private life. Until you came in. My life has been blown away, and now I realize how wrong I was to think I was weird. And If I was weird, dear God I love being weird. Those jawlines, and the smoldering eyes were enough to blow me up, but you looked like a fit lumberjack to boot. And like cherry on icing, you were the best human I've had the pleasure to meet. In just weeks I knew I loved you, if not immediately. But I knew I could not tell you, for losing you would've killed me. I was content with having you in it, as a friend or otherwise.

I have had many a conversation with you about my failing relationships and my inability to love, and you've provided me with the same answer every time. All the while your only answer has been that there is someone out there better for me. I want to tell you that there's no one out there better for me than you. No one could care for me like you do. And there is no one I could love, like I love you. But fear still keeps me shut.

But soon I started seeing the difference in the light in your eyes when you talked to me and to others. You seemed genuinely happy with me. And your failing relationships with the fair sex was telling me a story I was all too familiar with. Were you too living the same lie? I asked myself with the most neutral mind I could possess. And the answer was leaving me breathless. I had to know. I soon enough I did.

Some stories need a divine intervention to start off smooth. Because we as a society have given so many people different starting points to the same race, that people do not realize how lucky they are, until they just aren't anymore. And God did bless us that evening. Stranded from the group during the annual trek, brisk rains out of nowhere, just enough space for two to stay dry. It was a story scripted by the best of angels.

Sharing just a cubic foot of space, keeping each other from getting wet and getting themselves wet in the process, we both knew we were not going to walk away the same after this. And in that moment, I knew the answer. I knew what was in store for me, for you, for us. And in that deep embrace, I found everything I was looking for.

And everyday since then has been a roller coaster ride with you that I am willing to ride till I die. Hiding from questioning eyes, evading questions regarding our whereabouts, eloping for out quiet dates where no one would question why the oddest couple was sitting together. Those risky trips to our small heaven made all the lying and risk worth it.

I realize how messed up the situation is, when two adults are forced to hide their love for the sake of society, which is messed up in its own innumerable ways. I want to confide in our closest friends about us. And I want to celebrate everything that makes you, you. Given the chance I would scream from the tallest of peaks about everything I love you for. And I am ashamed that we are not playing our part in normalizing love. And I will have to live with that guilt in my heart all my life. But I pray with every fiber of my soul that one day, some young kid with fire in his heart and a will to defy and change will have the courage to do what I was so scared to. But for sake of not losing you, I'd carry that guilt to my grave.

And as I rest my head next to yours, so many years gone since the fateful rainy day, but not one bit of the love has changed, I wonder to myself.

Is us being together such a sacrilegious sin, that the world would rather see me with a gun in my hand, and not you?

Is our love so different, that our photoshoots trouble more people than serial killers do?

And if it, how is our love different from the cute girl and the good-looking boy 3 seats behind us? And why are heads turned away from us, and they celebrated?

I may never know, and I never hope to understand why people would feel that way. For in you I found my life. What do people have on me, when I am with you at the end of the day. In the bustling restaurant, with all our friends, some in a relation, some as single as possible, I reach across for your hand, as you slide yours over to me. But at the last possible moment, we stop. Ever so close, and yet so far.

But in our cozy café, when it's just you and me, over a couple books and a hot cup of coffee, we hold hands. Just us together. And I feel as whole as I could ever feel.

- Rohit Praveen

97. Post Its

"I love You" read the green post-it note stuck to the fridge, reminding me of you every day.

—

I've been forgetful my whole life and heavily relied on post-it notes. Keys, wallet, cell phone, documents, you name it, I've forgotten it. Over a while I started getting a reputation for it. Soon from materialistic things to dates, anniversaries and birthdays, my forgetfulness knew no bounds. And as my reputation preceded me, I started losing friends too. No one wants someone who can't look after himself, picking up all over after him.

—

But I remember the evening when I finally asked you to move in with me, after dating for 4 years, focusing not only on love but also on our work, making enough for us to plan out our lives. Interesting enough, I remember the day I asked you out. It was a scene out of a movie, slight drizzle and yet the sun out. A seemingly perfect rainbow studding the parking lot while we sat on the hood of a car, picking out its colors. I remember your face, initially scrunched in disbelief at the boy with commitment issues asking you out, then the realization that we were meant to be. I was the happiest man alive.

—

I also remember the day I knew I was going to marry you. And how exactly the next day I asked you to. You said yes without losing a beat, and I thought I couldn't be any happier. Marriage blessed us, kept us together through debts, a pandemic and whatnot. And in 3 years we have our first child. Oh, the nerve-wracking week still brings about chills. But we were ready, with our pup and baby, my heart was as full as it could be. For sure, my heart was running out of space to love.

—

I was wrong. The second brought me happiness beyond measure. And in our cozy home, I found my world. Watching our kids grow in front of our eyes, from cute little toddlers, to curious pre-teens and to insolent teenagers, they grew up in a flash. And so did we, as did our lives. Moving on to a lavish villa, taking in more pets, getting promotions we didn't dream of, and yet still loving you the same every day. Life was giving me more than I could ask for.

—

My memory is still bad. Forgetfulness seems to be an inherent part of my life for which I have no answer. I forget so many things that you're afraid I'll forget that I love you. And so, you stick a post-it note on the refrigerator, inscribed I love you, changing it every month. And yet I remember that your favorite flowers are white lilies, and how you hate anything spicy for breakfast. I remember to tell you every night what you mean to me, in case you were worried about my memory.

—

The years went by, and life flashed past. The dreaded day came upon so fast, it caught me blindsided. Our kids were moving out. Ready to face the world, equipped with everything they hope would help them. I see a bit of myself in them, in how unsure they were of how they'd react to life. And I see a bit of you, in the determination that they'd overcome no matter what. And with them gone we moved back into our cozy home, with the last of our pups.

—

You need glasses to see and can't thread the needle like you used to. I joke that you're getting older, while by back aches every time I bend to pluck the weeds. You get sick, you survive. I get sick, I survive. The sticky note now is a ritual. A reminder of all the things we've been through, and yet the love remains. The beautiful garden which we made with our own hands host birds of different kinds. I wake up to heaven every day.

—

I wake up one morning to the sound of sweet birds chirping. I wake up to the smell of fresh grass, covered with dew. I wake up to the sun peeking through the hills, sunlight seeping through our window illuminating your face, radiating a heavenly glow. I wake up one morning. You don't.

—

It's been a month; the sticky note is about to fall off. The green post-it note, reminding me that you love me with all you heart. The house collects dust, since you left, I haven't touched a broom. Our kids check in every other day, they love us so much. It's been a month since you've left me, and I'm still reminded of your love. And as I sleep at night, I see my life flash as I close my eyes. I close my eyes, and let myself slip into the night.

- Rohit Praveen

98. Halfway There

"This distance is getting to me", we both said it at the same time.

And rightly so, this long-distance relationship wasn't for the weak ones. When you got the fancy promotion you've been eyeing on for years, there were few men happier than me. But when the promotion letter read that you would have to move 400 km away, my heart sank into an endless pit, or so I thought. But the job was far more important than convenience, and since we both earned more than enough for us, it wasn't very difficult finding you a perfect place near your office.

Oh god I remember the first week, it was the most chaotic and bipolar week I've had. It gutted me the day you left for work. I felt like someone just reached down my throat, grabbed my small intestine, pulled it out of my mouth, and tied it around my neck. And I did not have my best friend to chime in with "Cookies?" And just as quick I was ecstatic with every one of your calls. Within the 3rd week we realised stability is a state of mind. You need to be close emotionally, and the lack of physical proximity becomes less of an issue.

By the 2nd month, monotony set in. And it took us by surprise and our relationship by the scruff. We were fighting over the smallest of things and me, being the insecure one, had the worst-case scenario planned out. And to bring in an element of surprise, I took up guitar lessons without telling you. And when I sang you my first song 'Hey There Delilah' I could see the sparkle in your eyes like when we first started dating. 'Hey there Delilah, don't you worry about the distance, I'll be there when you are lonely', made so much more sense!

But soon enough the guitar tricks became repetitive, and you could only cook so many exquisite dishes with household items before the boredom sinks in. The days change, but the conversation doesn't. Same old quarrels, but now getting more frequent and less logical. We were tiring each other out unimaginably fast, and our happy moments were being slowly overtaken by ominous sad memories, fights and whatnots. And I've heard this story before, and I didn't want to be on the wrong side. So many stories about strained long-distance relationships which wither away with neglect. And even though we did everything we could, life became unbearable by the 6-month mark. But I knew you had your vacation in a week and I was as impatient as could be.

But life was never easy on us. When you said your vacation got rejected because of the huge influx of patients, I knew this might put a new level of strain on our relationship. But deep down in my gut, I knew I would not let the beautiful bond I made over 7 years fall to pieces like this. It meant a lot more than an angry video call wanting to end things. And with that in mind, I planned the best way to win you back, like old times, to come visit you, and reclaim your hand.

And for planning something of this magnitude without you on my tail was an impressive task. But with the benefit of hindsight, I wonder whether I was living in your plans too. When I said that I wouldn't be able to call you for 2 consecutive days, you had the wily smile I'd recognise in my sleep. But I paid little heed to it, because I was pre-occupied with planning for my surprise visit. And it would not plan itself. I needed to book our dream car, pack enough things for a couple of days, and you know how irresponsible I am at that. But deep down, I knew something was amiss with that smile of yours.

I delved into our memories to pick apart everything and find out the most personal one for you. And all I could think about was the trip we never took, always postponing it to a future date, which now seems improbable. How fun would have it been had we taken the trip as planned. But lamenting about the past yields nothing other than guilt and regret. And so, I decided to recreate the trip with the destination as you. I packed everything I had to and set off to see you, and possibly to the best surprise you had in a year.

I took off into the evening, deciding to drive through the night. The cool air hitting my face, my hair flailing around and falling on my face, having the radio play my favourite songs. I felt alive for the first time after you left. But it only made me realise how much more I'd rather go with you, having the rooftops down, belting to random radio songs and living the best life possible. All in good time, I consoled myself, all in good time. Taking it slow, driving well below the limit, taking ample breaks, I was having a stroll. Until I reached halfway to you.

As I pulled into a restaurant, I thought you would've liked; I saw a car so similar to yours; I swore I would've guessed it was yours. And just like that, I brushed away that thought and moved on into the restaurants. And as always, I went for the seat we always choose in every restaurant. The one which has a fan closest to it, and probably closer to the kitchen. And to my dismay, the seat was already occupied. By whom, was the biggest surprise of all.

You were sitting there, alone, hunched over your phone, still making sure your office was running smoothly. Your hair pinned up in a ponytail to make sure it doesn't disturb you while travelling. Wearing your travel clothes with POCKETS, so you wouldn't have to depend on me. And completely lost in thought until you saw me. And in your eyes, I saw everything I missed out in the past year. And in our deep embrace, I knew I found the person I wanted to be with for the rest of my life. It was always you.

- Rohit Praveen

99. About the writer

About the writer:

Rohit Praveen

Rohit Praveen is a 20 something introvert, found usually sipping coffee and mulling over a Spotify playlist. He loves Love, Romanticism and Sarcasm, in no particular order. Takes a while to open up, but will feel like home, and till then warms you up with unrelated stories about love.

100. I Say I Write

i say i write to touch
the hearts of millions
but i write
to make myself feel
anything but empty
i say i write to make
people believe in
things unknown
but i write
to make myself believe in
all the things i don't
i say i write to help
thousands fall in love
but i write
to make myself
fall in love with me
i say i write to feel
the adrenaline in my veins
but i write
to get rid of all the pain within
i say i write to heal
but i write to numb
all the pain i feel

i say i write to lift
people into the sky
but i write to make
myself feel lifted
i say i write
for others
but i write
to make myself whole
i say i write
but i all i do
is bleed.
- Jess Doshi

101. Perfections And Flaws

people ask me how I fall in love so easily. there are moments of silence between us when I hear your heart beating and the soft sound of your breathing. there are moments when you're drunk and crying out all the secrets you had never let out. there are moments at 4AM when you call the people you love with a bottle of vodka in your hands as you pour out your gratitude for them. there are moments when they wake up and don't know where they are and their eyes look lost. there are moments when they let out a soft sigh cause something disappointed them but they didn't want people to know. there are moments like this everywhere. and these moments of absolute honesty sprinkled with admiration for a friend make me fall in love. I don't fall in love with perfections. I fall in love with flaws. and if you're already in love with the flaws, the perfections can't stop you at all.

- Jess Doshi

102. They Asked Me To Write Poetry

they asked me to write poetry
but all I could write was
love's cruelty
they asked me to write love
but I touched the topic
with hands in gloves
they asked me to write flowers
but I could only write of
Rapunzel's caged towers.
they asked me to write hearts
but I wrote of empty shopping carts
they asked me to write bold
but all I could write were
stories untold.
they asked me to write moons and stars
but I wrote of abandoned cars
they asked me to write romantic dates
but I wrote of broken and
rejected mates.
they asked me to write oceans
but all I could write was
unnecessary human commotion

they asked me to write you
but that was my leaving cue.
they asked me to write
but all it did was
take way my might.
- Jess Doshi

103. Love Taught Me

Love has taught me many things.
But if I had to note down 5 of them,
I think they will be this.
It scares me that when people ask me
About love,
I write about the heartbreak.
Instead of the endearment.
Sometimes two amazing people meet,
See galaxies in each others' eyes
And let go of their insecurities.
But the timing is wrong.
Their stars aren't aligned,
And what once bloomed slowly, wilted away
Despite how real it felt,
That is how the cards had been dealt.
It is the broken hearts that lead the world.
The combination of soulful pain and mind-numbing feelings,
Is the most powerful of them all.
Imagine a world,
Where broken hearts never were a thing.
Where love was widespread and
Hate existed nowhere.
What is the purpose of a world like that?

The word 'love' isn't just associated
With some sort of romantic involvement.
What about the time my father silently hugged me
While I sobbed and sobbed until I couldn't breathe?
What about the time my mother shed tears
Watching me cry over someone who didn't deserve me?
What about the time my siblings silently gave me space
Without me asking for it?
But worst of all,
Love taught me that pain is silent.
That heartbreak doesn't have a voice.
That you won't hear your heart cracking into a million pieces.
That despite how loud the music is, you can't run away from
the memories.
That the steps of the person you love
Walking away from you,
Is the only closure you will ever get.
I still believe that when a spark ignites
Between two people at the same time,
They should make a run for it.
Chase their love and destinies,
Carve their niches in the world.
So don't lose hope,
It all works out.
Because baby, taking a leap of faith is better than taking a leap
of doubt.

104. About the writer

About the writer:

Jess Doshi

Jess is an avid reader and a passionate girl. Her interests are not only limited to reading and writing, but also stretch far and wide to the environment. Through her writing, Jess hopes to make you feel things that you can't place! :)

105. The perfect painting

Isn't it frightening, how in one moment you could fall in love with someone. They say that about love at first sight but I find it so crazy how you could fall in love with someone, so much it could take you a lifetime to get over? In just one moment just by looking at them once. This person you see might become a huge part of your life or you could also never see them again but one afternoon when you pass by the same place it might remind you of them. Maybe we're destined to meet these people, sometimes we just get lucky, either ways this person becomes such a part of us or our memory that's too beautiful to let go of. A very uncertain start and an unfinished ending to something that might be an adorable love story or just a faint memory of a stranger across the street.Someone you might never see again but in that moment I could see galaxies in their eyes, the sun directly fell on them, turning into a silhouette of the most perfect shape the world around became noiseless, all other colours faded and you could only see them as if you could hear their thoughts calling you from the other side as if there were a spotlight on you maybe like a stage.With two characters you and them on different parts of the stage, at rest, looking beautiful, just like it were a painting, by the painter sitting in the audience painting in detail the tips of their fingers and every strand of you hair. The most perfect painting of two complete strangers from different worlds on one stage in awe of each other's beauty.

- Sanchi Jain

106. stars of kindness shine the brightest

there are so many human emotions that are usually reactions to the occurrence of something or that normally exist in us but empathy and kindness are ones that only you can bring out nobody can force that from within you. Doing big things is not what empathy and kindness is about, it's about the little things that we do that show us that we're capable of giving love platonically too.

it's about how you speak to a sick person how you treat a person who isn't able it's about comforting a person whenever they turn to you for comfort it's about wiping the tears from someone's teary eyes when they turn to you it's about treating them like you would treat yourself if you were sick it's about treating them like they're a part of you, treating them with kindness, compassion and empathy.

our days on this planet are numbered, everyday when you're kind to someone that kindness will always come back to you some way or the other because life is a boomerang and you get what you give, always.

so look at it this way each time you're kind or empathetic towards someone you accumulate a small magical star so within the numbered days you have, accumulate how many ever stars you can so that when you're gone, you put your starts together and become a big star shining bright in the sky a star that people wish upon. a star that someone out here will still always remember because when you were kind to them the little star you got was a piece of them that they gave you for a piece of you that you gave them as your kindness.

- Sanchi Jain

107. Magic

when I was a child
I used to believe
in castles and fairies and worlds undescribed
lies the magic in wands and trees from the other side
but now that I'm sixteen
I think there's more to magic than castles and trees
there's magic in a strangers smile
there's magic in my friend that I haven't spoken to in awhile
there's magic in my mom's prayers
there's magic in my sister's tears
there's magic in those flowers grandpa got for my birthday
there's magic in her eyes when grandma asks me to stay
there's magic everywhere I look
in people places and my favorite book
there's magic in your heart and everytime you're kind
that magic is felt everywhere just don't be blind
to love we were designed and what more magical
than the emotion that conquers all divine
just open your heart and let out the child inside you
it's a huge world you'll feel it too
- Sanchi Jain

108. Because I'll love you

I've never regretted a single time I've said I love you to someone, it doesn't matter if they said it back or not, it didn't matter if they loved me or not, it didn't matter if they knew me or not, it didn't matter if they've done me wrong, it doesn't matter if they're far off and we haven't spoken in months, it didn't matter if they didn't love me back, it doesn't matter if they love someone else more than me, it doesn't matter if they'll never be able to love me like I love them, it never did it never will, I love you because I do, there was something in that moment when you made me the happiest person even if it was just for a second, in that second I loved you and I said it and I'm happy I said it, because that moment will never come back, you might never come back, I might never be there again, we might never see each other again, but I loved you then and I will hold on to that second that I only loved you, and when I remember you, when someone mentions you, when I see you, I will think of that moment, I loved you, I'll love you

- Sanchi Jain

109. Realisations

Why are you not happy
Why don't you take a look around
Why don't you be grateful
Why don't you live
Why don't you say thank you
Why don't you be nice
Why don't you why don't you realise
You've only got this one life
say thank you to the store guy
play with sister like you're still ten
go and give your mum a hug
Go tell your girl she's your love
you're only human
stay humble be kind
you might not live forever
you might not live for long
but you're living right now and that's what counts
Be happy it's your one life
And you might not be able to do everything
But cherish every memory you got to live
it's time to realise, it's time to live a real life
No one has a perfect life
But everyone has only one.

110. About the writer

About the writer:

Sanchi Jain

Sanchi is very creative and prompt, she loves reading books
and is a huge fan of romance novels. She loves watching
romcoms, she loves singing and gets randomly excited. She's
the kind of person that'll look at pretty skies and be happy.

111. Cadaver

The cadaver lying on the hard mosaic floor, with it's nonchalant dead stare -

Demands that liberty be finally granted to it.

The imprint of all tragic plays, still vividly visible on that cold wrist sings the final lullaby.

The now wrinkled blackish - fuchsia lips permit the heaven sent stale air to deposit on it -

And the ears helplessly wait till the never ending replaying sounds of despair and dissection finally disappear.

The soul rejoices though -

For now it won't recognize the same old smells of horror and pain that the nose frequently inhaled , anymore.

But deep inside, there once resided a heart that pumped and a brain that fantasized about jocund days ,where the waist length ebony hair would swing to the rhythm of an invigorating atmosphere.

But,could this fate have been prevented ?

Perhaps even Nostradamus would've been unable to envision this :

The fate that supposedly terminated the ongoing journey of this cadaver somehow, as events unfolded and led to it.

But converted radiating beings into living cadavers instead :

Who now dangle in the threads of a permanent bereavement.

Because, a death is never about the beings that cease to exist -
But certainly about the bonds that are left behind.
- Aneesha Roy

112. Privilege

Let me lament one last time ,
How infuriating it is to spend a dime -
For people like us who love to whine,
Why everyone isn't just as privileged and fine –

–

Every time I express resentment over
not possessing that lustrous apparel ,
A girl , not afar, in her torn petticoat runs embracing tightly a
piece of bread,
yelling she possesses a soul that's not so frail.

–

Another friend of mine-
while adoring his guy,
gets bludgeoned into submission by peers ,
who believe displaying affection for the same kind shouldn't
be accommodated in this sphere.
While I, filled with guilt still joyously shout –
How me and my guy aren't queer.

–

Next, I quarrel with my mom,
when she interrogates and intrudes my only domain –
Just then the scream of a teen my age fills the atmosphere,
Who gets pummeled to the ground for playing with her

brother's new lyre.

—

I know not how to be more grateful
For now that I'm acquainted to the truth.
The suffering of unprivileged people in ruth;
Whose hearts display imprints of torment and fear –
Must disappear.
- Aneesha Roy

113. An open letter to my younger brother of 8

No.

Masculinity is not superior and being feminine doesn't automatically get translated to being weak.

Blue for males and pink for females.

This is not the default.

Craving to wear and experiment nail polishes of various colours is not a crime.

Stop talking to women in a condescending manner.

You might've been conditioned to learn and behave in this ridiculous manner, I understand that.

But fighting off this ingrained preconceived notion in your mind, is up to you.

Choosing to be rational is up to you.

The next time you yell -

"I despise makeup and dolls, even touching them by mistake makes me unholy and less of a man "

I'm going to disown you.

And whenever you judge females for wearing their desired apparels -

Think that's evil and immodest of them -

Imagine how it would've been if the socially constructed gender roles had been reversed and you couldn't wear your favourite tshirt.

Any materialistic or physical attribute doesn't define a woman.

Short haired,

Long haired,

Or bald -

Hair has no pivotal role attached while analysing a woman's character.

Last but not the least,

Always remember -

Women are no less than men.

- Aneesha Roy

114. About the writer

About the writer:

Aneesha Roy

Aneesha is a high school student who's currently in the 11th grade. She would describe myself as an insatiable bibliophile who believes life is too short for completing all the savoury books that exist. She defines Poetry as a language that transcends beyond this created binary by humankind. This language has helped her express herself and brings her relief.

115. At night

What keeps you up at night?
I was up late thinking about his sight
In the middle of the night
Honey brown eyes
A wonderfully sad smile.

–

What makes you not sleep at night?
The ordeal of sleeping still
An incubus under the bed
Hiding in the darkness of the night
And as soon as I switch off the light
It becomes alive.

–

Why are you not sleeping yet?
Not seeing the nightmare you should have seen and be fret
Avoiding the nightmares
I stay upright at night
Playing songs on repeat in my mind
Acting like it won't cause any strife
Taking long strides
And staying up at midnight.

- Apurva Kumari

116. Break Apart

Hold me close, share same air
You still feel far away
Can't make things clear.
It's blurry outside
The tears cloud my eyes
Cheeks felt damp
And mind felt numb
Can't hear your voice
It's too damn far
Hold me close, don't break my heart.

–

Can't say a word
But I feel it all
My mind's so full
With an aching heart.
I'll hold you close
Will make you laugh
I won't let go
With a breaking heart.

–

The blizzard in snow
Won't keep us apart
Stay this way

Don't break my heart.
It effing hurts
We can't fall apart
Hold me close, it's too damn dark
Can't see the light
So guide me past
I can't see anything
It's too damn dark

—

Take my breath
Tear me apart
Can't see you there
In the dark
I'm soo numb
And it's dark
Can't find you
We fell apart

—

You say you love
You say you care
But I don't feel love
And you don't care.
- Apurva Kumari

117. Portrait of a lady

I'm an imagination. A mind and soul trapped in a body of illusion. I'm a creation, someone's mind's deterrence. Most illusionistic likeness of a mother, sister, daughter, aunt, wife and grandma. But these things don't define me cause at the end I'm mere a being, a human being like yourself trapped in this body, an image painted by the society. But my soul is genderless and it knows nothing less than just love. Not the love of a mother, sister, daughter, or wife but the love beyond all. Self love. You try to shame me cause of my gender, paint me red because you believe I've no color. But how ironic that this body made of nothing but blood and flesh is noting but me as I'm red. You say you want no part of me that I'm filth an abomination in the society because I'm not capable of protecting myself, containing myself. You say this but I need to protect myself from no one but you. I can't contain myself because you won't let me because you also know you don't want me to have a mind or a soul but just as a furniture in your home. But you who is made of someone like me, a woman, when separated from me there remains noting of you. I'm your mother, sister, wife & daughter but I'm also beyond your imagination. I'm a portrait of a lady.

- Apurva Kumari

118. About the writer

About the writer :

Apurva Kumari

The name Apurva means 'something which did not exist before or is newly born' and she tries to abide by it spreading the commonly different ideas and thoughts and still believing in the impossibilities that the future beholds for us all. She believes in art, literature, words, moon, romance and every earthly thing ever created by the nature.

119. The homesick window

Sitting beside the window,

I reminisce about the long-lost love.

There's a certain fragrance in today's air.

It reminds me of the time when we were so happy and full of life.

The purple haze sky unlocks the nostalgia locked deep inside my heart.

When we used to roam sleeplessly in the night, carefree.

We were two opposite forces,

But when we were together, we would make the forces of the world rise.

And made all the passerby conspire.

I wonder where these thoughts disappear.

I look at the sky and wait for a shooting star to make a wish for you.

Will the wind blow in our favour?

Will the sky cry when we leave?

Will the road beg to hold our steps?

But now the dawn has come near and you're not here.

—

So i wait with my pen and paper in my lonely chair.

Accompanied with the memories of you to keep me alive.

- Tanveer Zaman

120. Maudlin Moon

Accompanied by the sound of the waves and illumination of the moon,
I breathe my misery away and take a look at the horizon.
As the lonely boat retreats I close my eyes
and feel the cold breeze and wish for it to take me
and fly me away with the wind as I become nothing and everything at the same time.

- Tanveer Zaman

Chapter121

The night is long
And the soul is weary.
Destiny is far away
But the day after that is cozy.
The well is deep
And the water too scarce.
Wait for your patience
To nurture a fruit that is rare.
Drink from your cup
And quench your thirst.
Don't go to the dry land
and be unjust.
Remember the Almighty creator
For he has a place for everybody.
Face your battle fearlessly
For a never-ending glory.
Make your vision clear
and be ready.
He has come to your doorstep
Don't turn away, open the door
For this is your story.
- Tanveer Zaman

122. About the writer

<u>About the writer :</u>

Tanveer Zaman

Tanveer Zaman was born and raised in the city of Kolkata. Tanveer has faith and a passion for cultivating new ideas. In his poems, Tanveer paints a picture of his imagination. He picks on the curiosity of the reader and portrays how past events can be turned into something creative for a positive outlook.

123. The night is hunting

The night is hunting and the emotions are the hunters,
We remember some people and some we try hard not to remember,
But the mind keeps running on thoughts, we cry we play we laugh harder,
The wind is cold and the feels are getting colder,
You are trying hard to sleep
but the mind keep reminding you how hard it's to keep the track of the number,
The number of times you gave everything but you got nothing in the name of love,
The number of times you said you didn't expected anything but all you wanted is they Never make you feel alone,
Alone? I guess everyone's alone with their journey,
it's just the people who take a part in the life
and leave it without saying goodbye,
Cause it's easy to run from what you feel instead facing your real fear?
But that fear will hunt you at night and they will give you the nightmares that you will remember.

- Sikarvar Krutika

124. Ruka ruka sa vaqt hai

Ruka ruka sa vaqt hai, or araman bekarar hai,

Chote se dil me khwahise hazar hai,

Par kya kare khwahison se pet to bharta nahi?

To fir Dil ne kie kuch tikhe se kam hai,

Har kam me khusi dekhne vala dil ka ab rakhta ye dimag hisab hai,

Ek nahi do nahi teen nahi na Jane karta dil kitne saval hai,

Jo pasand hai vo pass nahi,

jo pass hai vo pasand nahi kabhi kbhi lagta hai

akhir is dil Ko akhir kis par aitbar hai??

Kuoro ki tarah man nahi leta ye

Dil dimag ki bat akhir ispe konsi aisi khurafat savar hai,

shayad dimag ko talash hai paiso ki

or dil ko har roj kuch naya krne ka khumaar hai.

Par dil aise khwahise Puri nahi hoti

tumhe karna vahi hai jo dimag ki taraf se ho chuka hai,

rakh de apni khwahison ko or kam pe tu lag ja,

Kal ka suraj agar khusi khusi dekhna hai to dimag ko rakh tu sath or dil ko bhul ja.

Jo pasand hai tuje use jane de or jisko tu pasand hai uske sabr ka imtihan na le,

Kar le thodi choti chize jo kare tuje sukhi ku ki inke bina zindagi hona ya na hona sirf ek saval hai.

Ha dil ki ye umra hai choti par is bawre ki khwahise hazar hai

Khair chodo is pagle pe akhir kis ko hi aitbar hai?

- Sikarvar Krutika

125. About the writer

About the writer :

Sikarvar Krutika

For me writing isn't not my hobby it's my lifestyle, I can write anytime anywhere. I love to stay in imagination where I can make up my own stories and can tell people how I was feeling while writing that story.

126. The Life Sailor

Just like a sailor sails
Even in the most turbulent weather
Even after losing some co-sailors
Even after leaving behind those lovely villagers

–

The Villagers
Who enrich the sailor with experience
Who aid the sailor during turbulence
Who provide the sailor with shelter
Who nourish the sailor with fodder.

–

Just like the sailor sails
The journey of life prevails
The tides take us away
Adding memories along the way

–

The Memories
With an ocean of people we meet
With a sea of personalities we greet
With a river of lives we touch
With a pond of friends we clutch

–

The Friends
We learn from and we teach
We gain from and we give
We build with and we break
We forgive and sometimes we even forget

–

Then again some day
Those memories shine
Like the treasure the sailor finds
Meanwhile
The next village seems to be in sight
The next set of adventures shine bright
The sailor adjusts the sail
Ready to write yet another tale.
- Swetapadma Narayani Acharya

127. A Smile I Am

A smile I am
That lights up your face
After the darkest of days
Through the tears in your eyes
I emerge as a victor fighting all lies

–

A smile I am
Who fights all hurdles
Fills you with strength through your troubles
To convey that you will win
You have the courage within

–

A Smile I am
Which can transmit in a second
From one kind face to other
Whether they are unknown or a friend.

–

A smile I am
That brings twinkle to your eyes
When the dress you wanted fits your size
That brings joy to your soul
When you smell your favorite food and you can't control

–

A smile I am
Who brings peace to your heart
When you see me start
Curving the lips on their face
'Coz you were better than the people they met

–

A smile I am
Which makes you thrilled
When your parents have me
Marking your success in your field

–

A smile I am
That everyone deserves
That gives you pleasures
That is full of treasures

–

And I promise you to stay
To fight your battles along the way
Till the time you cherish me
In these tiny little moments everyday !
- Swetapadma Narayani Acharya

128. About the writer

About the writer :

Swetapadma Narayani Acharya

An enthusiastic girl hailing from the temple city, Bhubaneswar, with a keen interest of diving deep into human thinking, thus pursuing Psychology Hons. With a love for food, songs and literature, she seeks her daily dose of motivation from spreading smiles around her. She believes that our actions and accomplishments speak in volumes about ourselves and thus strives to do her best.

129. The world is a Masquerade

Each day you wear a mask,
hiding yourself from others.
Too insecure from the truth to embark
the journey that wrecks the zones of comfort, that bothers
you and all the sheep around.
So you wear a mask and
hide the truth underground.
Making the world a unique Masquerade,
With you and sheep dancing
a meek rigid dance, round and round and round.
And you call the different a sinful soul
hiding under the mask you call, the amour of God.
You envy deep inside to those who are naked
with no truth and lies.
As you know you are dead inside the
mask that suffocated the lives
of millions who chose the easy path, wearing a pall
making a world a unique masquerade ball
with that meek rigid dance.
So go round and round and round.
- Raunak Singh

130. Life

Life, what is it?
A journey so musical
Or the Pandora's gift.
Many come and go
finding its meaning for ages
Many tried to explain it like the seven stages.
But do we really live?
Is the question so far
Is life is just a so called suffering
Or bliss at the altar
With we in the puppets play Playing our roles
dancing around the center
Being the center all along
So play by your own rules
make the choices you want
it may be not be simple
But it will be worthwhile and your own.
- Raunak Singh

131. About the writer

About the writer :

Raunak Singh

Raunak is an introverted person who likes spending nights alone under the shade of full moon and an open sky full of glitery stars. He loves painting, writing poems, reading and writing fiction about supernatural and life, death and society. He loves freedom of individual and appreciates divesrsity among people.

132. Dear younger self

Dear younger self,

I miss you. I miss your presence.

Yes, I miss being myself. I miss those days when I was used to be cheerful and happy,I knew what i wanted, I used to listen to my heart and most importantly i had a solution to all of my problems.I miss those days when eating and sleeping were the only two activities i did. I had a clear and transparent mind then.Almost every little thing around me provided me a tint of happiness.

Well,its not the same anymore.Things have changed with time.Now,my mind has been cluttered with endless amount of stuff.I don't know what i want from life. I am clueless about everything.Now,everything is so puzzled and blurred.

Sometimes, I wish i never grew old. Adulting is making me feel lost and insane. I don't feel myself anymore.Everyday, when I wake up there is something going on inside my mind.I don't remember the last time i smiled happily. My life has become dull and monotonous. Sometimes, I think i should get a break from everything and chill but that never works.Everything is so unpredictable.Sometimes i just wish to disappear and i feel no one would be bothered by my absence. I love collecting souvenirs. I don't collect them anymore. I just sit with my collection and go back to the flashbacks. I remember how chirpy I used to be earlier. I used to attend all social get-togethers and parties and meet everyone with a jovial face. Nowadays, I just look for reasons to avoid any kind of social interaction. Earlier, I used to be optimistic about everything but now my mind doesn't let me think anything positive.

But you know what? Maybe all this is just a phase. Maybe, i'll get over it soon and feel myself again. Maybe I'll get to know what i actually want to do in my life.

Maybe I'll find the solutions to my problems again. Maybe I'll start collecting souvenirs again. Maybe I'll start meeting people again. Maybe I'll be happy again.

Maybe everything will get better with time.

Maybe?

—

- Saswati Vaniprava

133. Wo pehli baarish

Garmi ka mausam tha.Charo taraf bas loo chal rahi thi aur log pasine se lathpath ho chuke the.Pashu-Pakshi paani ki ek boond ke liye taras rahe the.Ped-Podhe paani ki raah dekhte-dekhte murjha gaye the.Main aur mere parivar ke sadasya balcony mein baithkar mausam ka halchal radio pe sun rahe the. Achanak se mere chehre par ek boond paani gira.Maine upar dekha kahin chhat se paani toh nahi tapak raha.Phir jo ek ke baad ek paani ke boondo ki barsaat hui mere dil ko jaise maano thandak hi pohanch gayi. Gagan me badal nritya karne lage.Sara parivar khushi se jhoomne laga.Ped-Podhon ko jaise jaan hi mil gayi. Mitti ki wo anokhi khushbu soongkar mann ko tripti mil gayi.Tabhi dadi adrak wali chai aur pakode lekar aai.Humne chai ki chuski lekar pehli baarish ki khushi achhe se manaai.Kuch der baad baarish ruk gayi.Pashu-Pakshi apni pyaas bujhane lage. Aasmaan ki taraf dekha toh ek aakarshak indradhanush nazar aaya. Wo khoobsurat drishya aaj tak meri aakhon mein sangrahit hai.

- Saswati Vaniprava

134. The girl at the shore

She smiles like the sea full of spirit
Her presence is like God's gift
Her hair colour is blond
Wandering here and there like a vagabond
Every now and then she's in my mind
Oh lord why did you make her so kind
She smells like fresh chamomile
Her heart's so pure and full of life
Spreading smiles everywhere
She walks towards the shore with no fear
Fire in her soul, tipsy are her eyes
Am so in awe of her, still in surprise
Sunrays falling on her face
She symbolises serendipity and grace
Suddenly she comes towards me
I am not able to hide my glee
"Will you click a picture of me?", she said
Spellbound by her I nodded my head
As she poses, my adrenaline rushes
An alluring scenery my eye catches
The camera fails to capture such beauty
I feel blessed to witness this deity
The way she runs her fingers through her hair

I can't stop looking at her and admire.
She walks through the waves like an angel
While I wonder "Oh lord, is she for real?"
- Saswati Vaniprava

135. About the writer

About the writer :

Saswati Vaniprava

Saswati loves long beach walks and evening hues. She's an
avid reader and often gets lost expressing in her writeups.
With a passion to experience the beauty that lies outside her
comfort zone she's always ready for it with the right song.

136. My eulogy to myself :

My eulogy to myself :
she passed away eating her last fries,
at the age of 203,
Left her belongings to her dogs,
That's the way she wanted to leave.
she was reckless, unbreakable, and fierce
like her poems,
the poem where people leave her,
much more than they loved her.
she was a careless fool,
fell in love with him,
knowing it'd set her on fire.
she wanted to itch poetry,
on snow-capped Mountains,
with words that turn,
a shy shade of pink,
the color of her palm
when she pinches tightly.
she was the shattered piece,
of the glittering moon,
hanging in the night sky,
reflected in the midnight ocean,
in liquid gold.

poetry was her hiding place,

where she was paper-thin,

her fears are the,

howls of many wolves.

how pain made her open the temple of her

heart,

and allow hatred to walk in,

wearing wet, muddy shoes.

she was made up of apologies

and unsent letters most quiet,

hiding in the quietest corners of the room,

overflowing and gleaming out of every slit.

(I want this to be read when I'm on my death bed)

- Sanjana Seth

137. The one that got away

your absence is becoming a habit for me now.
your absence
tastes like old coins swaying inside my mouth
but I started finding peace in it.
thought it was just a phase,
but now you became my lyricist.

–

your presence was home
but now I fear difference
I can weep alone, but I think
I will go numb in your presence,
I told you lights makes me happy,
but darkness is now my comfort zone.
since you're gone,
I let my mind take me,
someplace new as long as,
it's a place I haven't been with you.
your love was the worst hangover,
I ever had
pretending to be sober
realizing still not so over,
to dance in the doomed brace.

–

I write poetry,
on broken people.
wondering if you are broken,
or is it me who's broken?
remember,
you always loved it
when I wrote to you
keep writing,
you said
now I wonder if I'll ever be able to stop writing about you.
maybe not,
because this is my way to show
that I'm heartbroken,
you bring out all the poems in me.

—

I wouldn't say that I was surprised, no
I saw it coming
I saw that you had her clenched inside of your fist.
being with you was locking myself away in a room.
And haunting my shadows convincing myself that it was you.
I'm afraid if she dips the straw,
drinks all our memories from your eyes.
don't make her eat the poems
that I wrote for you. (the one you loved)
- Sanjana Seth

138. Loving you is like

Loving you is like -
chewing gum staying for 5 years in my digestive system,
sticking to my heart and getting caught in my ribcage,
for more time than you deserve.
increasing my anxiety day by day and
With that my grumpiness,
Reaching a point where I feel it heavy in my heart and fraud
in my smiles.
The falls season,
the leaves fell and so did I
Fell apart thinking about you.
Drowning,
I never learned how to swim,
All I learned was to use my hands and feet,
And When I met you my hands and legs were tied. Blooming,
when you smiled at me
But now becoming one of the thousands of thorns of cactus.
Living in dungeons toxicity,
It's sad coming out of it never ends.
Making my soul soggy,
Like a wet napkin after a cup of coffee has fallen in love with
the floor.

some days I'm not so fond of myself because the night you broke my heart I ended up turning my anger into poetry.

- Sanjana Seth

139. About the writer

<u>About the writer</u> :

Sanjana Seth

Sanjana is a law student halfway to her 20s and she's over it. her spare time is spent writing poems and listening to angry music. she loves chasing sunsets and sniffing books, living on an unhealthy dose of movies and cold coffee. she can turn anger into poetry.

140. Wrong routes

One impulsive decision was all it took for me to change the direction of my legs.

I took a wrong route,

And look where it got me.

I emerged from the tree cover. The gentle tugging the breeze did to my loose shirt felt like nature's way of affection, almost like it appreciated my exploration of its glory.

I looked up to the sky and the frenzied pulses sent out by my heart pounded so hard at my chest.

The yellow ball of fire changed to hues of orange, and then almost tangerine. It merged with the sky, like juice-mix dissolving in a glass of water. The clouds were cotton-candy, as though they blushed at the warm touch of the sun. Silhouettes of birds flew home across a sky that was now magenta; and the sun was half into the water, but its reflection in the sea made it look complete.

The sun, threatening to dip behind the horizon, firstly cascading a hue of colours that were flung over the sky. The receding blue and oranges battled the blackness pushing it away with arms. It shone on the sea below shining its deep depths. The radiant glow beamed.

The sunset is merely a prelude to the dawn, yet its majesty fills my mind with the most beautiful of dreams.

Wrong routes take you places,
Places that you'd never find.
Take a wrong route,
And see where it'll take you.
- Eashita Raj

141. Nostalgia

Though we can love our traditions, of dresses, suits and rings, the realisation happens long before in the quiet moments of the star-united lovers.

"When was it that you realised?" He asked while walking towards me.

"Once upon a time is such a cliche start to a story," I laughed a little, "but here we are."

I peep outside the curtain and sigh. It had started raining. Which means one thing - mud. Lots and lots of mud. I switch on my phone for the hundredth time and decide it is better to arrive early, rather than make him wait in the rain. I grab my faded sports jacket and leave my house. The building is deserted, but I feel intensely conscious as I navigate around the pools of water forming in the pothole-filled road that leads out of the building.

Suddenly my mobile vibrates hard and I almost drop it in shock. It's him. He is already at our 'adda' - the local xerox shop, where we have spent many nerves racked evenings, getting last-minute printouts of notes. I realize my palms are slick with moisture. It could be the rain. I know it's not.

I turn the corner and spot him, standing lightly, one hand holding a blue umbrella and the other clutching his redshirt. He looks like a breath of fresh air, and I feel my heart beating faster, and my ears turning red. I smile shyly at him and he laughs.

"Kitna sharmati hai yar tu!" He laughs and pulls me towards him. I just buried my face in his shirt and grumbled out a "shut up" while he continued laughing. He waved an auto and fifteen minutes later we were on our way to Nariman Point.

Sitting in the auto is never a good experience with untied hair. My hair was all over my face and I was trying to brush it out of my face, when I turned to look at him he was smiling at me. "Aise kyun dekh raha hai?" I asked, feeling conscious.

"Sundar lag rahi hai." He said while kissing the side of my head, which had the auto driver giving us nasty looks but he shrugged it off.

We reached Nariman Point and by then the rain had stopped and it was dark with the city lights in view. The moon was bright and the stars were shining. I knew this was going to be an epic night.

We go to the side and sit at the edge facing the waves in the front. I grab his hand and move closer to him, intensely aware of our arms touching each other. The next hour is a series of poor attempts at humour from me and a lot of his dazzling smiles. We planned on watching a movie but then decided against it. This was our favourite thing to do- just sitting here and talking. I felt his arm snaking itself around mine and pulling me up. He curled his fingers in mine and gently rested his head on my shoulders and snuggled in, while engrossed in telling me about his day.

"Achha, ek random question," I said and he lifted his head to look at me. "Laati kaha se hai tu random questions?" It was a rhetoric question. I looked at him and asked. "Why do you love me?"

He tightened his grip, pulling me more snugly in his embrace, "Because you bug me weirdo. Duh." I chuckled and sniffed a little. "Sometimes you're too close to someone to see what they really are." I said.

"Sometimes you love them so much that you don't want to." He said, pulling me closer and continued, "I've never been so scared of losing something in my entire life, then again nothing in my life has ever meant as much as you do."

I looked at him with my eyes wide open. "Hain kya!" He cradled my face in his hands and said, "I can always count on you to come up with such reactions. Yaha main apne pyaar ka izhar kar raha hoon and tu hain kya bol rahi hai." I gave him a sheepish smile.

"Arey arey! I'll love you forever paagal!" I laughed and he pouted. "Naah, ab tune moment kharab kar diya mera." I shook my head and laughed. He cradled my face in his hands, wiped the tears away and said, "Want me to continue telling you reasons? Because I can go on forever." I smiled fondly at the memory. I looked to my side and there he was standing beside her, holding her hand. "Kaha tha na, I'll love you forever." I said nudging him. He smiled and kissed the side of my head and walked with me towards the Pavilion.

- Eashita Raj

142. About the writer

About the writer :

Eashita Raj

Eashita Raj is a law student who has been raising awareness through her writings since middle school. She obsesses over biographies of famous people and is an avid reader of many genres. She firmly believes the major driving force within herself comes from penning down her thoughts.

—

–

143. Wallflower

In a world full of flowers, I'd rather be a leaf. When the flowers are trying to grab everyone's attention, I'd rather blend in with the surroundings. Sure, there's nothing special about a leaf and there are thousands of them to the point where everyone looks the same. But they have a very important role to fulfil and they do so in the background. People might say that a leaf will never catch someone's attention and it's better to be a flower but, there are some people out there who notice the blandest of things. Wouldn't it be nice to have the attention of someone who's really interested than every other person?

- Samruddhi Prashant Kamble

144. I told the stars about you

Dear love,

I wonder if there are people like me out there, who have open conversations with the stars. Be it a heartfelt sob story or a joyful one, I'd tell them all, they're just wonderful listeners you see. I sometimes wonder if they chatter amongst themselves about me and my stories, if they make fun of me or sympathize with me. I'd never know… all I know is that I find great comfort in sharing little bits of my life with them.

But these days I feel a little uneasy talking to them, ever since I met you. Because you my love look like one of them- bright and beautiful. Whenever I'm around you, I feel the same level of comfort as with them. But that comfort is short lived because you see, one look at your eyes and I feel like they could see right through me, no holds barred. Don't get me wrong, ever fiber of me is in love with you but, I'm scared. I'm scared that you might already know that I'm not so special, scared that you might know of my insecurities, and everything that I hide from the outside world. Scared that the stars might've already told you about my unrequited love. But I still hope that you'll choose to stay despite knowing all of it. That's where I feel like I'm getting too ahead of myself. I'm just an average girl after all. Like a tiny cloud passing by, easily forgotten.

Despite all these doubts and fears, I still thank the stars everyday for giving me a chance to have met you. And I think you know that too because you seem to know almost everything on my mind. I've gotten so used to your presence that your laugh echoes in my mind every time I watch the stars twinkle. Now all there's left for me to do is pluck just enough courage to mail you this letter or toss it into the pile of letters all addressed to you underneath my bed. Probably the latter, but if somehow this letter manages to reach your doorstep, please know that it took me a great deal of effort to do so and that I'm strong enough to take whatever answer you have for me.

With love,

A hopeless romantic.

—

- Samruddhi Prashant Kamble

145. About the writer

About the writer :

Samruddhi Prashant Kamble

Samruddhi loves listening to vintage music and spinning tales around them. She likes sketching and can be found jamming with her guitar on a lazy day. She believes in the power of classics and her stories tend to recreate that long lost magic.

146. Reasons

I cannot recall all the reasons,
why I fell out of love.
The 12 AM calls when you are slightly drunk
And playing xbox with your mates.
You would still call to tell me about how Rohan made
sandwich with bread and kheer.
I giggle a little, while you whisper into the metallic device of
how you miss tugging my drenched curls.
Maybe, it is the 2 PM video calls when you are in class and I
ignore because,
I was busy watching the re runs of a new show I just found.
You don't tell me how your day went,
And I never bothered to ask.
We meet up every weekend and laze around in a bookstore.
Were we afraid to talk to each other, or were we just enjoying
the silence that made home between us?
I watch you from the corner of my eyes as I take a long drag
from my cigarette.
I notice how your hair was now brown and that you changed
your glasses.
You stopped wearing your mother's ring around your neck, it
now gracefully hugged your finger.
I remembered the nights, you used to wake up screaming,

How I used to calm you down, like a lost star in a forest of embers.

I cannot recall all the reasons

Why I fell out of love,

A bundle of letters lay on my couch unread.

Maybe, you write too much.

Your feelings all pushed down in a paper that I never picked up.

I pick up an alphabet which you plucked from the first typewriter you owned.

I realise that it was among a bunch of other things that you gifted me.

Other things-

You preserved the napkin on which we played tic tac toe while listening to ABBA.

The X's had started to fade away.

And the dried flowers from our first trip to Ladakh which I had forgotten to keep inside my diary.

Everything seemed out of place.

I cannot recall all the reasons,

Why I fell out of love.

I watched the trees on our way back home that night,

Nodding lightly to me as if they understood my pain.

I stand outside my house,

I bid a small goodbye and wish you the best.

As I watch you drive away,

I rush to my balcony, hoping for the leaves to hug me tight.

I cry and cry into the night,
Realising,
I cannot recall all the reasons,
Why I fell out of love.
- Blue

147. Comfort

This was comfort for me ?

until you left me shattered in ways?

only the sky could understand. ?

I waited for the stars to burn out,?

for ours was a love that could?

never exceed the walls which I built safely around the cigarettes and the 3 AM conversations. ?

I'm holding onto every part of me ?

that believed in man made stories ?

of her prince charming. ?

I'm holding onto the whispers, ?

I've grown used to ?

when you think I'm asleep. ?

I'm holding onto every colour?

I've used to paint?

a picture, so blurred ?

that you laughed at it. ?

I'm holding onto ?

You, ?

You, who wished for a fairytale ?

but got a goddess with broken wings. ?

You, who seemed to wander with the wilderness, ?

turned into a home for a lost wisp. ?

You, who started giving into, ?
a lie you were hiding behind.?
And I'm still here, ?
holding onto your shadow ?
with my, ?
scarfed fingers, ?
struggling to let go.
- Blue

148. Tales

I tell pa to begin again.
To tell me about,
all the machos in their love stories.
How Ma ran towards him with daffodils just wavering.
He laughs at my generic love story.
This was his favourite fairytale,
and my ultimate love goal.
1970s was a miserable time for Ma.
The beatles were disbanded,
The emergency period was a bracelet for their love capsule.
He stops mid way,
asks me, if she ever thought of marrying him.
This was their inside joke.
I tell Pa to begin again.
This time the story is a bit different.
He forgets ma's name,
he makes up for the latter by cracking a limerick.
Then I wonder, if theirs were the love story,
I wanted to live in.
I pour him, his two shots of whiskey,
He said, ma could weave poems out of his drink.
He finishes it in a gulp.
The guilt ridden look,

his trembling fingers,

the droppy eyes,

they were the heroes in my adrak chai.

Pa says he heard the doorbell,

I walk out of his room,

glancing at the blue blanket drapped

over my mother.

The guests had brought friends,

Pity and sympathy.

But I didn't know why?

I go back to Pa,

urge him to begin again.

Only this time, it was a confession.

He said, he wanted to be the wind that never slowed.

So, he ran where his scars took him.

Hid where his blood ran muddy,

And killed when his eyes grew dark.

He came back,

with a hand to write and a foot to run.

He came back,

when the poetess had destroyed herself in a whirl of suitors at

night.

He said he craved her,

when the couch had space.

He wanted a new story,

A love story, he was in.

So, begin again Pa.

I said,

and succumbed to his dominant tongue.

- Blue

149. About the writer

About the writer

Neha Ann Jishnu (pen name Blue)

Neha Ann Jishnu (Blue), pursuing Masters in English. She is an occasional poet, avid reader, connoisseur of chai, and art, and a romanticized observer.

150. Call of the Blue

I stand in the field
With my arms stretched wide,
I take down my shield
And I've got nothing to hide
For the blue's calling me

–

I lay on the cold earth
Beneath the roof of stars,
Nothing but joy and mirth
And so I reveal my scars
'Cause the blue's calling me

–

I stand atop the hill
And scream with all my strength,
I'm so full of thrill
From head to toe's length
And the blue's calling me

–

Here I am on the bank
of a river unknown to me,
watching as the sun sank
agreeing to the moon's plea
And the blue's calling me

—

I take down my shield
And I've got nothing to hide
Because the blue's calling me now.
- Rashi Rajgor

151. Mystery

Oh she's a mystery alright, one that keeps you turning pages
that will calm you down
But bring out your rages
She is the moon that you gaze at and prayer she shines her
light on you
But she pulls you in her craters
She is the cherry blossom and a look at her makes you numb
Epitome of beauty in the spring
But more admirable in the autumn
Honey she is the flower Whom, from harsh winds you prevent
It will soon give you the fruit
But she's got you drowning in her scent
There's just one way to love her
And that's with all your heart
And with all her scars 'cause darling she's a mystery but are
you ready to tear yourself apart?
- Rashi Rajgor

152. A lifetime per day

I felt sad one day
thinking about how
people are completely okay
with living only one life
and I was like hey
I want to live thousands
so I picked up a book next day
which took me to golden rivers
and lands made of clay
I saw owls flying wildly
and unicorns running astray
I saw winged creatures
getting in a fray
I learned to laugh and cry
and for more I'd pray
I learned how to keep
bad influences at bay
I made some cool friends
with whom I'd play,
and with whom I ran around
on a field of hay
I loved beautiful souls
and in my heart they stay

so I don't know how
you can be completely okay
with living one life in a lifetime
while I live one per day
- Rashi Rajgor

153. Healing Hurts

I still feel at a loss for words when I think about the number of feelings that were exploding inside me when he got down on his knee. I thought every moment from that time onwards would make me feel just as what I felt when he asked me to marry him. It felt like I was flying headfirst into something big and it tasted sweet, like cotton-candy and it smelled like I was in the midst of a meadow. I never wanted to leave. It's weird how easier it is to describe feeling something, in tastes, and smells, rather than in words assigned to those emotions.

But if I was to feel like that - like being in a meadow, euphoric, all the time, what would be the point of living at all? And yet, if I had the choice of feeling no other emotion than happiness instead of feeling this hollowness, this void inside of me, I think I'd choose happiness. Because at least then, I'd have someone to share that happiness with. But whom do I have, to share this bitterness with? And so I'm writing this story. To feel a little less.

I think I should have known it would never last, we were both awfully green when this journey began. I was a little more than seventeen when we first met, contemplating theories about Time Travel, sitting around that small table in the public library. I had come in to get some books for the upcoming Economics test and there I had seen this boy, hardly eighteen, eyebrows scrunched and eyes attentively scanning the pages of, "A Wrinkle in Time" by Madeleine L'Engle. I remembered reading that book when I was 13. "Are you enjoying the book?" I asked the boy. He glanced up and looked around as if taking in his surroundings for the first time and realizing that he wasn't in the world of the book. I smiled at that feeling.

"Yeah, it's quite intriguing", he replied, putting the bookmark between the pages and shutting the book close, for the conversation. I felt honoured by this small action.

So I sat down in the opposite seat, taking in his appearance properly. His hazel eyes seemed to be doing the same. He had dark brown hair, not too short but not very long either. He had olive skin which blended with his features quite nicely. "Have you read this book before?" he asked, continuing the conversation.

"Yes, I read it when I was in seventh grade." I answered, in a matter-of-fact voice. "Now there's a way to make me feel insecure about my reading habits." He said with a laugh.

"Not at all. I don't think there is any certain age to read a book for the first time." He raised an eyebrow at this statement as if asking me if I really thought that. I simply held my serious expression.

"Well in that case," he said, glancing at the book again and back up at me, "I guess I ought not to feel too insecure" and he flashed me this goofy smile that felt like chocolate melting on my tongue. The rest of the details of our meeting might be blurred but I remember that smile vividly.

I get out of bed and make an effort to go about my day as if nothing had changed. And it hurts, but I try not to dwell on it.

"How will we make it work?" he asks me, anguish in his voice.

"I don't know... We'll find a way, won't we?" I reply, hesitantly. My eyes search his for some kind of assurance. Instead, I just see what I dreaded most.

"I'm not sure anymore, Eve."

Eve. His nickname for me. I walk around town thinking about how warm it made me feel every time he said my name. Just the one word from his lips, acknowledging my existence made my heart soar. And how it absolutely broke me when he said it a week ago. The last time we saw each other. I make a right turn two blocks from my house and it cheers me up a bit to see that Arene's town High School is holding their Annual Fair. Teenagers milling about, trying as hard as possible to attract visitors to their booths. I walk around a bit, passing my time in hopes of distracting myself.

"Would you like a ride on the Ferris Wheel ma'am?" a boy, about seventeen years old, asks me. He is probably the one who has the responsibility for this booth. "Yes. Sure, I mean" I reply, thinking it over. It could maybe help, a ride on the Ferris Wheel. The view from the top would be a bonus too, since it's dusk. I pay for my ticket and get in line.

"The town looks so beautiful from here, doesn't it Tri?" I ask him as we were sitting in one of the seats on the Ferris

Wheel in the neighboring amusement park. He didn't like the nickname I called him when we first started dating, so I insisted on calling him by it just to see that cute look on his annoyed face. He eventually warmed up to it and that same heart-meltingly pretty smile would adorn his face, the same as the first time we met, every time I now called him Tri.

"It is. And you know what else is beautiful, Eve?" he asks. "The moon?" He laughs and shakes his head. "You knew I was going to say 'you' and that's why you said the moon, didn't you, you sneak." I joined him in the laugh and then he kissed me. "But you're prettier than the moon, Eve." I kissed him right back and the butterflies I felt in my chest fluttered as if there was no tomorrow.

And I remember thinking how perfect we felt together. The dark twinkle in his eyes when he said, "I love you" for the first time that evening. And how I didn't hesitate for a second before saying, "I love you too, Tristan." I miss him. The tears threaten to spill from my eyes and I quickly wipe them on the back of my hand. "No," I think, "no no no." I can't afford to cry in public. Here, amongst these teenagers who are having the time of their lives. I get down from the Ferris Wheel and walk back home. It's dark now but it's barely seven in the evening. The humid breeze rushes past my face and I'm reminded of our last conversation. "Hey Evelyn" Tristan gingerly called me out from the study. "Yes Tri! I'm in here," I answered him back with a shout. At the time I was just finishing up adding another shelf to my bookshelf. "I think we should talk for a bit" Tristan said in a serious tone which made me stop the hammering for a moment. "Can't it wait until I've put my precious shelf up?" I asked with a chuckle, in an attempt to lighten the mood of the room. "Don't make this harder than it needs to be Evelyn." Tristan sighed and walked up to me where I was sitting on a chair in front of the bookshelf. "You called me Evelyn twice. You never call me Evelyn," she says, with a slight shake in her voice, "even when we fight, you always called me Eve." "Listen, Eve, please. I'm sorry I don't know how it's going to work anymore, you will be miles away from me and-" "Are you breaking up with me?" I cut him off before he could speak more. Tears were starting to form in my eyes. "Eve, you got a job on the other side of the country and I already have a good job here which I cannot afford to lose. And never would I ask you to leave such a good career opportunity for me."

"But we would make it work somehow, wouldn't we? Just tell me we can work it out James, please." I was begging Tristan with tears, now wetting the carpet the study. I felt so little and pathetic in that moment but I couldn't help it. I tried but I couldn't.

"Don't you think I've thought about this Eve? I have! I don't think we can work this one out. The distance would kill us in a way worse than this." Tristan said, the anguish in his voice clear as a bell.

"But I-" "Please Eve, don't. I know what you're going to say. I would miss you terribly too. I don't know how I will get on without you but this has to be done. It has to be. Please understand." Tristan pleaded, holding both of my hands in his. We both stayed in the position for a while. Crying silently in the study. "I should leave now. Goodbye Eve." Tristan said and walked out the study. As soon as I heard the main door click I collapsed on the ground and cried myself to sleep. I woke up and saw the half-done work of the shelf. "I can't pull my life together just about now but I can put this shelf together." With that I started up and managed to add another shelf to the bookshelf.

- Rashi Rajgor

154. About the writer

About the writer

Rashi Rajgor

I'm 16 years old and currently studying at St. Xavier's College, Mumbai. My literary inspirations are Jane Austen, Sylvia Plath, Franz Kafka, Virginia Woolf, Roxane Gay and Mary Oliver etc. I aspire to find a career in writing when I grow up.

155. The Spirits of the lonely Graveyard

"Greetings, listener.

Have you heard? About the blue and white spirits of a lonely graveyard.

There is a saying about it. If you walk into the graveyard at exactly twelve am and twelve minutes, you can see and hear their whispers....krrrrr" *crack* *crack*.

The old radio on my desk finally turned silent. My thoughts didn't. They still traced back to when I re visited the graveyard. "Dead Childrens are buried here" the English was so incorrect yet eerie in the way it was written. The handwriting seemed to be written by a madman.

The graveyard, creepy and aesthetic in view to cipher your mind on. Each grave was a child that didn't make it past nine years of age. I was there to visit my twin sister, Mariah. Eleven pm and fifty - five minutes, my Belle watch read. Today my freshly red tinted shirt made me escape home and greet her, finally after so many years. I miss her more than anything. Her grave still brewing fresh Jasmine flowers. Her favorite.

Each grave grew different ones. That was the most eerie fact for me. But I wasn't the only human to walk this graveyard. I glance and see a familiar face sitting next to a freshly buried grave.

"Offer love and comfort when you can. Do that for me, brother" I'd do anything to keep you alive Mariah.

I tap on their shoulder and motion if they needed company or wanted to be left alone. Twelve am. My watch beeped. The grave had dandelions growing around it. The human now sat peacefully ,softly hugging me from behind for comfort.

Twelve hours and twelve minutes, the graveyard lit up like fire in the woods. Each soul penetrated out of their graves like a phoenix rising from it's ashes. The graveyard did wonders on one particular lunar eclipse once in 7 years. The souls stretched, danced, sang and talked about how their relatives visited them or how they like their afterlife friends better. If they are aware they are dead.

I never bother them, I dare not to talk. Even to my blue little sister Mariah, for my skin knows where it has been when you dare speak to the dead.

- Haru

156. Words do Wonders

"It doesn't count if you're already planning defeat ya know" He whispered to me.

"But. I don't stand a chance" I responded, fidgeting my bandaged fingers.

"But haven't you been trying hard my friend? You look like you have been practicing Archery all day and night! They aren't some aliens on the arena. They are humans just like you" He said with that freckled smile on his face.

It gave me courage. I don't know what wonders happened, but it filled my anxiety with ease and confidence. He was right. They are humans too, 16 year olds like me. I have worked hard and so have they.

"You are right. I shouldn't be running away" I got up with my bow; my head held high as I thanked my hippie stranger for the words of confidence.

And then. I never looked back ever running away from a war again. The words fueled my will power like match stick to gasoline.

- Haru

157. About the writer

About the writer

Ananyaa Sharma (pen name Haru)

Ananyaa (Haru) often can be seen listening to music and reading books on their laptop. They like doodling and can be found researching on random topics at any given moment. They believe that words have powers that are equivalent to magic in books.

158. Silly Maze

Leaves shedding from trees.
Flowers are blooming again, its a sign.
You were standing under the tree,
Looking at me, it was wrong but felt right.

Days went by, can't forget the moment.
I am looking for you everywhere.
We both are lost in this crazy world...
Its like a maze, try your best.

We both are going to find each other,
Someday or in a year.

Silly Maze
It goes round and round,
No space to escape, we are stuck.

Lonely nights
Its getting dark,
There is no escape, Baby run!

I was looking for an outlet... But a voice called me,
I was so confused and about to kickback but,

The hope to meet you hitted me.
Looking for you eagerly with no clues.

I am not going to leave you alone,
No matter how hard it gets... I will still find you.
The maze is getting closer, a hint was seen...
The maze wants to cram our love.

We both are going to find each other,
Someday or in a year.

Silly Maze
It goes round and round,
No space to escape, we are stuck.

Lonely nights
Its getting dark,
There is no escape, Baby run!

Silly Silly Maze,
Goes round and round, we both are roaming in circles.

A sharp beam of light was coming,
A figure was created... Coming towards me.
It was you! We hug each other.
Your scent covered my body.

Silly Maze
It goes round and round,
We both met each other.

Lonely nights
Its getting dark,
Now we are going to live happily ever after.
- Pihu Sharma

159. Crazy Love

The disco ball is going crazy,
Like the drinks which makes me daisy.
The place is full of drunken babies,
Do you wanna leave the club maybe?

—

My eyes are only stuck on you,
Like the drinks which makes me blue.
Do you wanna dance with me too?
Or you can be my option two.

—

Your eyes are giving me a curse,
Like the witch who made me the worst.
My legs are moving towards you,
Is this a dream which comes true?

—

Every night I think about you,
Next day I fall for you.
More and more, Just for you.
Love me or I am a criminal too.

- Pihu Sharma

160. A walk in the woods

Under the dark light of the moon,
I was going to enter the woods soon.
Scary but adventurous it saw,
Real but Imaginary it was.

—

The moon was shinning so bright,
They were going to come at mid-night.
The imagination was hitting way hard,
They crawled and made their way out.

—

It was hard to breathe,
They were suffocating me.
The imagination is hating me,
Their presence were faking it.

—

Time was passing by,
My world was cramming down.
Trying not to get scared,
Their power was coming now.

Saw the monsters they were,
Getting on my nerves... It was there!
Got locked in this cage in my Bay Hut,

They are coming so near.

–

Only fear that we have,
It's Imaginary... But scary.
A walk in the woods,
It was my own imaginary fairy.
- Pihu Sharma

161. Losing the moonlight

The bright light of the disco ball itched my eye.
Sparkles falling everywhere, it was someone's turn to say goodbye.
People dancing on the floor, made the night high.
Little did she know, it was time for her vidai.

–

People flattered as she made her way divine,
The last stare of a father made everyone cry.
Never wanted to leave her house, it was destined.
An innocent soul left her memories behind.

–

"Aishwarya!" an old father's voice cried,
Remembered the time when he first heard her cry.
Never wanted to see her absence from his sight.
Kissed her forehead and said her goodbye.

–

Her small steps made his memory rewind,
The day she said "papa" was dying.
A father's worst nightmare was coming alive,
Sending his daughter away was a sign.
- Pihu Sharma

162. About the writer

<u>About the writer</u>

Pihu Sharma

Pihu Sharma is a high school student who loves to write about events she imagined or went through. Her imaginations are like a sky, never ending. She is an Introvert and loves to spend most of her time alone. She also loves to write short stories, songs, listen to music and dance.

163. Opportunity

As am sitting on the windowsill
The cool breeze hits my face
And I get lost in those dreamy days

—

The days when I was challenged by my strength and
capabilities
When people believed I couldn't
I believed that I could
When everyone tried to low my self-esteem
I was getting ready to go upstream

—

I worked hard to achieve
They kept pulling me down
But I was too determined to let go
Cause I wanted the gong

—

I took their challenge as an opportunity
To prove myself
I turned it into an opportunity
To improve myself

—

Letting them say what they wanted to
Because it's me that matters the most

–

Suddenly am snapped back to the reality
With the gong that worth infinity

–

Those memories worth more than 24 carat gold
cause when we'll grow old
we'll have a smile on our faces while rewinding the moments
so pure.

- Manya Krishna Srivastava

164. One last time

The lights went out
The stories are out In are the dark clouds.
Wish we could rewind Back to the time
When everything was right
Wish I could take back those words said in fury
Cause now i regret and my eyes are teary
I wish this is just a bad dream
Cause you were my only ray of beam
Now that you're gone
We are left behind to mourn
And i wish I could hug you tight
At least for one last time.
- Manya Krishna Srivastava

165. About the writer

About the writer

Manya Krishna Srivastava

Manya krishna srivastava is a passionate dancer and a literature enthusiast. she writes poems so she could tell the world how she actually feels and does her bit in changing the world by influencing people with her thoughtful words. she believes in being down to earth and helping out people.

166. Maybe

Maybe that wasn't our end
We felt love even before we knew what and how it is,
Our story ended before it could even start,
Maybe that wasn't our end.

–

Maybe our paths will cross again in a library among old
stained books,
Our eyes will meet, our hearts will reconcile among the lustre
of silence
And that is when we will feel love, again.

–

Maybe we will start off again,
Our fingers will curl around, the grip in our hands will tighten
this time
And that is when we will feel love, again.

–

Maybe you will hold me again,
we will lay entwined in each other's arms.
While I gaze at the gleam of the distant stars, you look into
my sparkling eyes, lean every once in a while just to kiss me
on the forehead.

–

Maybe you will drop by my place again,

To surprise me,

with flowers and a bottle of champagne in your hand.

We dance in the kitchen to our favourite song for the twentieth time while you lift me up and I cry my heart out

And that is when we will feel love, again.

–

Maybe we'll share our tales of love with each other again,

while I fall asleep in your arms, snuggle down cozily to your kisses, just to wake up to them.

And that is when we will feel love, again.

–

Maybe we'll start off again,

As I rewrite "maybe", my hopeless love for you just makes my heart even more hopeful.

- Pratiksha Mishra

167. I've seen people hide their cowardice under the sheets of melancholy

One day you'll look back, with a heavy heart, teary eyes and you'll wonder "what if".

–

What if you had seized that moment, grabbed my hand,
and we would've danced to our favourite old classical romantic tune

–

What if you had held my hand,
in the silence and eerie of the street,
in the dim light of the moon, the other night

–

What if you had kissed my forehead,
the last time I hugged you,
weeping quietly on your shoulder

–

What if you had tried closing your eyes,
to forget the world around you,
drown in silence,
just to picture us watching the sunsets together through our balcony every evening.

—

What if you had chosen to break the silence that night
and not two hearts, in absolute love.
What if you had decided to give it a shot instead of walking
away with nothing more than the heaviness of silence, pain,
numbness and tears to carry.

—

I've seen people consumed by sheer guilt and repentance
I've seen people hiding their cowardice under the sheets of
melancholy
I've seen people hiding tears underneath the redness of their
scars

—

And you, my love, is the last person I wish to see like that.

—

Yet, I know, you'll look back and wonder "what if"
- Pratiksha Mishra

168. The epiphany of my alter ego

The movie ended,
he smiled at me,
I placed my glass down
and we talked about,
true love.

–

As we walked out of the hall,
gazing lovingly at me, he went down on one knee,
my eyes reflected the lustre of the dazzling ring,
which fit in my finger as beautifully as his fingers fit in;

–

I cried like no one saw,
and we danced like no one watched
then, as I took a step forward to kiss him,
felt something ringing in my ears, vigorously

–

And
I opened my eyes,
15 minutes past 3,
the clock said.
slightly moved to silent the buzzing phone,
the littlest corner of my heart hoping it would be from you,

but
it wasn't.

—

Hopelessness, despair, misery
slowly crept in
my body ached,
wherein, your every touch, resides.
The walls painted in the hues of forlornness,
echoed my despondent shrieks,
hyperventilating my whimsical desires, causing
the epiphany of my alter ego.

—

My arm crave for yours,
while yours hold her
my eyes search for yours,
while yours found her
I fought for you, while you fought with me.
I found my ending, where you found your beginning.
I was ready to give up on everything for you,
while you gave up on me.

—

Little did my heart know that I'd be nothing to my
everything.
- Pratiksha Mishra

169. I can just dream of you

The window panes trembled, vibrating vigorously to the sound of the lightning; as silence crept in, the raindrops felt louder than ever,
two hearts, completely in love, yet too vulnerably delicate to call it love, went into the depth of a painful void.
As I looked up, caught you looking at me, my heart skipped a beat, the chords got disturbed, love tiptoed and we smiled.

–

Our eyes met through the slight gaps between the old dusty books,
as our hearts inclined towards the path of love;
Your fingers touched mine while you leaned forward to pick the very same book I'd been wanting to read to;
the way your fingers perfectly fit in mine, just make me drown in the intimacy of love.

–

The moment we picked our straws up, and began drinking from the same glass just so our foreheads could meet , my heart danced to its favourite beat of love, making my forehead crave for your tender kisses.

–

And as I opened my eyes, this dream, which felt better than any reality ever has, subsided, faded, slowly, leaving room for hopes.

–

I have seen the moon, the shining stars but all I wish to see is you and the luring beauty of your brown eyes.
I have felt the breeze, the fresh water running through an old stream, yet all I wish to feel is your presence.
The beauty of sunsets, the fragrance of fresh roses and the blaze of grey clouds don't soothe me as much as your arms do.

–

You're that beautiful dream, I saw with my eyes wide open,
Your heartbeat is the music I could peacefully sleep to every night,
Your gentle kisses are what I wish to wake up to every morning.

–

I'd forever move in the direction where your breaths, heartbeats move, and settle in there, lost in your eyes, crazy in your love, without ever regaining my senses, for the rest of my life.
You strike the deepest chord in my heart without even using your hands,
you make me laugh the loudest without even cracking a joke.

–

And as I feel every feeling beautifully, my heart dwells in the moment of helplessness, desperately wishing to tell you how lovingly it loves you, screaming how it lost and passed millions of moments to win over the enchanting magnificence of your love.

- Pratiksha Mishra

170. Letting go

You see, Letting go is never easy,
It isn't impossible either.

–

That tender heart of yours is craving for love, compassion
Like that little kid who's been looking for his lost candy, you
are looking for that lost piece of your heart.

–

You feel lost,
Like that little kid on his first day of school, you feel that you
have suddenly been dropped off at a place, you're unfamiliar
with,
you see a lot of people around but your eyes keep looking for
that one person,
like that little kid cries and screams, looking for his mother.

–

Every minute, a part of you is being consumed, a part of you
breaks every second.
All your heart wonders is if they're thinking about you too,
If their nights are all about you too and these are the thoughts
which torn your mind apart.

–

Every night you walk down the same dark path, beneath that
eerie green glow in the sky, all you get reminded is of the

time when you promised each other of walking down the aisle together.

—

In search of that lost piece of your heart, you have lost yourself, a part of you is alive, because of the excruciatingly heart-rending memories.

—

Your heart cries out in desperate grief, just like that little kid who struggles while looking for the last piece of his jigsaw puzzle, and that lost new born kitten who shrieks in agony, unable to see through the darkness.

—

Keep walking, for every road has an end, if not, a turning, definitely.
Keep walking, for the sun sets every evening, just to rise again, more beautifully, the very next morning.
- Pratiksha Mishra

171. About the writer

About the writer

Pratiksha Mishra

Pratiksha is a happy go lucky introvert who loves stargazing at nights and watching sunsets and believes that every feeling should be penned down beautifully.

172. Love letters to Bombay and a sporadic lover

i. i am tip-toeing in your briny fringes under translucent moonshine. instead of prancing back with sea-shelled nuggets, you drown me in the whites of your bedsheets. which is to say, you have planted salty angel-wings behind my eyelashes and i have become blind to your jellyfish bites.

ii. your love beats faster than a hummingbird living. your love is allergic to calm breathing. your love is five hundred cars crying. which is to say, every time i stall between two steps, you have travelled the earth twice already – you come back to me new, you come back to me foreign.

iii. we shed our skin cells on cheap gullys and colonial hideouts, and fall into manholes with liquored livers. i think ordinary sickens you. which is to say, every June, you either toy my frizz with your fever or choke my conscious with untimely flooding.

iv. i was on my knees when i saw you knitting multiverses. you bent time and space casually. your hands smelled of elaichi chai and buttered croissants. which is to say, you spoke many languages, had different skin; you slept at strange times, had asymmetric dreams – and i plucked out my heart and crushed it at your feet; i worshipped you for it.

v. i have seen the crowds that have built their homes on you. heaven hatches here, and with your neck stamped with topaz stones, this becomes a stampede kind of love. which is to say, i pump more of me into less of you, but you are never full. i ooze out sludge-like – the dredges of my arteries stuck to you.

vi. we are old–time lovers filtered through cinema lenses and radio tunes. we stole kisses behind cadillacs parked on moneyed streets and tongued like teenagers on lonely railway seats. which is to say i have scaled longitudes and latitudes running against/towards you and my blood is haunted with your fingerprints.

vii. bile has reached my molars and i still haven't finished writing about you. i gather all the alphabets and scripts i know, but they are falling short. they are falling short. which is to say, i will invent a language for you and someday, i will be enough for you.

- Jijnyasa Patowary

173. About the writer

About the writer

Jijnyasa Patowary

In every story I write, I untangle my mind's yarn.

In every story I write, I gather courage letter-by-letter to mark my being.

In every story I write, I sprinkle a little bit of my heart. When time engulfs us all, my words will carry on my legacy - isn't this beautiful immortality?

—

–

174. From where it fell apart

There was a day when everything was fine,
We both sat having some wine at a fine dine
It wasn't that , the fault was mine,
I never thought, i would whine,
It all ended up in an argument,
That was not supposed to be meant,
And from there it went to another level
It felt like someone just threw a pebble.

–

We both went away angrily.
I wish i could have handled it calmly,
Coz anger spoils it all,
Thats our biggest enemy afterall,
That was just the start,
From where it all fell apart,
I then just chose to depart,
And till now I can't get it out of my heart.
- Srishti Sinha

175. Confessions

I learnt one thing from life,

Confess before its too late,

Don't you just strife,

And serve as a bait.

Thats all i have to say to you mate.

It might be hard to confess initially,

But it isn't that bad,

Don't you think you are mad ,

Just give it a try and later you may not cry.

Its no use to later repent,

After all the moment you searched for just went.

You will at once become happy,

And, i promise it wouldn't get you snappy.

You will be just relieved,

If you just say it what you believed.

- Srishti Sinha

176. The Downfall

And it was the time of downfall,

There was no time to reball.

What do we do when something like this befall?

Do we give up? No, we don't.

We instead stand up.

Some won't but some will be by your side,

Then it all might just not collide.

Is it over? No it isn't .

Its just the beginning and we don't have to hover.

Don't give up and just rise,

I m sure you will be caught in someone's eyes.

And it won't be a time for any lies.

Many questions may also arise,

But there is no time for any cries,

I m sure, in the end you will all at once rise.

- Srishti Sinha

177. About the writer

<u>About the writer</u> :

Srishti Sinha

Srishti being an introverted person occasionally prefers penning down her feelings, emotions, and incidents. Usually her poems revolve around general things which we all face at some point of time. She really enjoys and admires nature and loves to travel and explore places.

178. Girl at the harbor

People forget years,
And remember moments.
They forget dates,
But remember lastingness.
But one waited there,
Standing at the harbor.
Days passed and months flew,
But she held herself for something new.

–

Tears never left her eyes,
And she never left a moment to smile.
Even, in her darkest days,
She waited for a candle to glow.
But her past has left on her some scars,
And now only old memories flow.

–

She waited everyday,
With hope to make some new memories.
Waited at the harbor,
Even when she reached the age of finis.

–

She died with prong in her eyes
Even in death, she only thought of her other half who died.

Her dauntlessness was still alive there,
As she waited for the one who never returned to wipe her eyes.

—

I heard her romantic chronicle,
I felt her cramp.
It took months for me,
But I completed my way of ending her prolonged life.

—

I drew a painting,
Oh her with her life.
With hands in hands,
Sitting on the bench, both crying.
Sun setting,
And they both dying.

- Diamra

179. Pain is a synonym of disease

With every passing summer this heart remains cold. It hardly gets affected from the warmth present around. Its so hard to not change when every little thing around you is changing. In this world of letting go, it's so hard to be the only one holding onto memories like your means of survival. Pain is like a disease. If you want to cure it, you need to suffer more to prepare the antibodies and I'm not scared of suffering but of still not being able to fight back.

- Diamra

180. Loving hard sometimes

Don't fall in love with people like me.
We will love you madly and you might leave us.
But with your departure our love won't cease.
Its meant to fly, not supposed to freeze.
The sky has both the sun and the moon
Just like the wind, we will let you bloom.
You won't be caged, you are meant to fly.
To see the world, to love before you die.
We won't make you promise,
We know they are meant to break.
We will align the stars for you,
We will love you for no one's sake.

- Diamra

181. About the writer

<u>About the writer</u> :

Diya Raj Gupta (pen name Diamra)

–

Diya is a 16 year old student always ready to welcome you with a grin. She loves the beauty of the world through artistic interests. She believes that where heart fails, words speak.

—
–

182. Metanoia

Blinding lights,
Traffic signs,
The recklessness of the youth,
Riding through the city of New adulthood,
Intoxicated by the air that feels so artless.
Don't we all get lost,
In this mad rush of of the adult world?
Juggling so much at the same time.
In the company of people,
Who won't be there for long.
It's scary for a minute,
To walk alone in the city.
But with time,
We all adapt to this new world,
That our lives get transformed to.
We all learn to let ourselves free
In this sphere that is so haphazard ,
And bloom into sunflowers,
That follow the sun,
Trying to shine as bright as it
But not getting blinded by it's brilliance.
We learn to set our ground,
And be the captain,

Of the ship of our lives.

- Vanshika Mukherjee

183. Déjà vu

Vibrant splashes of orange and pink across the sky,

Resemble a painting on canvas,

That I painted in my dream,

Is this déjà vu?

Or a waking dream,

That my heart longed for,

Name it whatever you want,

But to see this unfold before me,

Is a wish fulfillment for my heart.

And someday, I'll pick up my brush.

Make a stroke or two,

To capture this déjà vu,

And wish my dream, adieu.

- Vanshika Mukherjee

184. Heart: an Enchanter

A heart that beats,
Has a soul that grows,
Fights battles on its own,
Makes its strengths known.
The delicacy of the heart,
Is an unfathomable art.
A heart holds power, so gentle,
Yet so wily,
It could weave you into a web of love,
That you can never fall out of.
It breaks when people leave our side,
But still beats, like a broken record,
As a reminder that you have yourself,
Today, tomorrow and forever,
Even when they say forever is an illusion.
- Vanshika Mukherjee

185. Moonshine Blues

The moon is so lucky,
It gets to nap around clouds so soft,
Rest it's head,
And still stay aloft.
Fly in the sky jet black
And gift the children on earth,
Dreams of things so radiant.
I wish I could snap my fingers
And give the gift of light
To our lovely planetoid
Because it fulfills the dreams of millions
But still lives in solitude
In the unending black sky.
It stays hanging in the air,
For hours at end.
We murmur soft praises when it changes colours and sizes,
But never realize,
That those might get lost in space
The black empty space
Where the moon lives alone, so alone.
But then I cognize
Aren't we, the people,
The same as the moon?

We talk to each other, not letting our guards down,
Try our best to shine for our kinfolk,
While hiding our deepest fears,
And never letting them see our dark side.
Do you see how similar you are?
To the white pumpkin in the sky,
The one that you always look up to
But never comprehend
That you are the moon of your life,
The one who shines bright,
Surrounded by people,
Yet lone, so lone.
- Vanshika Mukherjee

186. Golden Rain Shower

Honey drops fall from the sky,
In search of the angels on earth,
To bestow upon us,
Blessings from the heaven above.
Threading lightly, the sky and our world,
To gift the humankind,
A second chance to be alive.
To wash away all our miseries,
And start our journey anew.
To ride away all the damage,
That cannot be undone.
The rain of honey brings with it,
A scent so wild yet pure
The scent of jasmine that allures,
All the mortal beings,
To assemble and take an oath,
To restore life into the earth,
Never cause harm to the ones around,
Spend a lifetime in peace, quite and everything tranquil.
And make an abode for all,
With a bit of love and heavenly magic.
For all the ages to come,
An abode where everyone is welcome.

187. About the writer

About the writer

Vanshika Mukherjee

.

Vanshika Mukherjee is an 18 years old high school student, she is the secretary of the Editorial Board at her school. She loves to write about nature and trivial things that often go unnoticed. She wishes to get better at expressing herself through words and wants to keep discovering new things about herself as she steps into the future.

188. Broken

I don't let the ink touch my diary anymore
because everytime it does it spills out a warm river of sadness.
and i've tried freezing it
but nothing helps.
it is as if i've let too much of everything in that now my room
looks messy.
and all i could do it just clean it up but it is in every corner
and i just don't know what to do.
but the more i leave it there,
the more it stinks.
it's funny how sometimes your heart doesn't allow you to fix
it.
you know exactly where it hurts. like walking up the stairs to
your bedroom and knowing exactly which step is broken.
but you don't fix it, you leave it there.
broken
- Aisha Chauhan

189. Perfect

all love ever did to me was make me chew all my nails.
and stay up till the time sun came up.
killed my butterflies and blamed it on my insecurities.
made numbness a path to home.
but i saw your smile across miles.
so warm as if i was wearing it.
your laugh so excited as if you just learnt how to ride a bicycle.
i tell you i don't want to fall because, love, it never ends well.
and you tell me love doesn't end.
you put science theories to define romanticism, and illustrate
why labeling love is a stupid idea.
you call me beautiful as i tie my hair right after waking up and
i feel..i just feel.
after a long time, i feel.
there you are dancing in your porch.
singing 'perfect' as the sun goes down.
and here i am, looking as your hair falls on your face.
i feel my heart skip a beat.
as if someone just handed me the perfect cup of coffee
- Aisha Chauhan

190. It's okay not to be okay

so its okay.

when you're head is hanging low because of the embarrassment you earned by giving a wrong answer in a perfectly hypocritical classroom.

and when you run to the washroom and its all empty while you expected a random smile from someone you don't know much.

it's okay. when you come back home and you don't have anyone to ask you how your day was.

it's okay when you can't tell anyone that you've been awarded as the best archery player in the school.

that 'awesome'mark on your essay given by your favourite teacher doesn't make you smile the way it did just half an hour ago. it's okay, it is.

it's okay when you're roaming around and you cant take out your phone in front of the guy who wanted your number cause you told him you don't have a phone.

and when at night, when you're playing with shadows and quietly whispering to your soul that you're not alone, its okay if you can't see your shadow smile.

the footprints on the sand don't stay the same when you return back, its okay.

its okay. nothing stays.

it's okay when you upload a story having pizza, captioning it with "this is real love" and you know that this 'love' is just going to fill one part in your body.

it's okay when you go to the bed and you think where would you choose to be if you only had 5 minutes of this air left.

and if the only thing that pops up is

Home. the home for your soul.

and even if all of this is not okay, its okay.

it's okay not to be okay sometimes.

- Aisha Chauhan

191. Ghost

scented candles,

half burnt, half broken.

sheets unwashed,

with your smell within.

shadows go through walls,

and my hands reach out to hold you.

but you never stay,

you never did.

it's been years and it still feels like yesterday.

you shook my hand in the hallway as I begged you to stay.

your broken heart kept breaking mine

but i was more resilient than you realised.

I didn't kill you,

then why won't you stop haunting me?

- Aisha Chauhan

192. Buried

that smile on his face,
when he felt like dying.
his hands,
cold enough to run chills down my spine.
strong enough to hold onto all the traumas,
but felt weak when he held me.
his voice,
bold and husky.
but couldn't even whisper 'stay'.
i tried to heal, touch, to feel.
punched his walls down, bruised my knees.
–

I still had his scars in my heart.
so i burried him,
and now his soul haunts me.
–

but I could never break his heart,
cause he never had one to begin with.
- Aisha Chauhan

193. About the writer

About the writer

Aisha Chauhan

.

.

A caring and passionate writer, singer, student who leaves a
trail of exhilarating, peaceful and contagious rush of
serotonin wherever she goes.

194. I tend to live in parts

I tend to live in parts.
Of joys and sorrow,
Lesser today more tomorrow,
With my eyes wide open at nights,
My moon has more than the sun's bright,
I lived upon and beneath the moments,
With my tangled hairs and dazed mind,
I try to fit in everywhere like the water,
With time I lost my flow,
I don't know where to go,
Said I was good at conclusions,
Now I'm down and joyous fusion, with time,
What do I call mine?
Oh, it's an illusion only in my heart,
Or all the way I'm falling apart.
- Sunny Prajapati

195. Run away

Run away
Throw it away
Past the day when it's yellow
Draw your goals and begin to feel them
Black clouds often create green grasses
- Sunny Prajapati

196. There were grasses

There were grasses and there were roads,
Dazzling sun and quiet sea shores,
Rhythms and blues in the darkest hues,
With all tipsy on some count of whiskey,

–

As we all leapt from the highest peaks,
We could possibly encounter our darkest griefs,
And turned them to our bleak of deeds,

–

Whatsoever we had in the time,
The drowning gold and the rising cold was our integrated dime,
We lost shame and pity, on the outskirts of our city,

–

I literally had a greatest of my times,
Writing and thinking our sunset point.
- Sunny Prajapati

197. About the writer

About the writer :

Sunny Prajapati

.

.

Sunny loves to read books and is anxious about art and science. Engineer by profession, writer by choice.

198. Tum ho

Tu woh sab kuch hai, jo mai tujh mai chahta hoo,

Tu ek aisa sapna hai,

Jo mai jeena chahta hoon,

Jo mujh raat bhar jagata hai,

Tu ek roshni hai,

Jo mere andhere ko jagmati hai,

Mujhe meri raah se milati hai,,

Tu ek tasveer hai,

Jo maine meri kalpana se banayi hai,

Tu ek aisa geet hai,

Jo mujhe bhitar tak chu jata hai,

Tu ek haqiqat hai,

Jo mujhe mere jinda hone ka ehsaas dilati hai,

Tu mujhse jyada meri rooh ko pehchanti hai,

Tu aajaad hai,

mere ander,

Meri aakhri saans tak,

Tu woh sab kuch hai, jo mai tujh mai chahta hoo

- Devsaab

199. Kagaz par shor

Kaagaz behtar hai,

panna dar panna raaj dabaye rakhte hai.. Sab sunte jaate hai, kehte kuch bhi nahi, Bas shyaai par shyaai nigalte jaate hai.. Ek band mutthi mai,

Lakiron sa reh jaate hai,

Kabhi panne fatt bhi jaaye, Tabhi raaj ander sama rakhte hai, Korre panne banke aate hai, saare raaj bharke apne upar le jaate hai. Kaagazon ke bas kaan hote hai, kaagaz aache shrota hai.

Kaagaz behtar hai,

panna dar panna raaj dabaye rakhte hai..

- Devsaab

200. Rakh hona chahata hoon

Main bajaye dhool ke, rakh ho jana chahta hoon. Main balki yeh chahta hoon ki meri chingari ek jungle ko jala jaye.

Mai balki ek shandaar ulka hona chahta hoon, Ek shandaar aur chamakta hua grah, Jo kaale aasamaan mai chamkta jaaye.. Manushya ka karya jeevan ko jeena hai, Astitva ko nahi, Mai unhe lamba khichne ke liye apne din barbaad nai karunga. Kya hoga? Kahin jaane aur pakde rehne ke bich, Hum phir se,

Ek baar aur pyaar ko jee paate!

- Devsaab

201. About the writer

About the writer :

Devend Sharma (pen name Devsaab)

Devend likes to travel. A charmer to people with a deeper perception of the world, penning down his journey called life.

202. Of goodbyes

Remember that evening?
When over a wine,
We were conversing,
That how one day eventually you have to leave?
For a different city, don't know for how long.
Since then I've been thinking.
Of goodbyes..

–

Of how weird they can be..
You & me, we know
That our story, is just gonna fill
Only some few other chapters of our books, yours & mine
& how floating in the air of the moment,
At the speed of wind,
how we just don't seem to care.

–

Of how struggle some..
When walking on an empty street,
Looking at the clicking clock
I would someday be thinking.
of how beautifully we spent the last few evenings at the same
hour
& then be fighting myself

to throw the thought out of my head.

–

Of how negligent..
Knowing that this moment in your arms,
This fragrance of you on me,
& of how I'll later be struggling
to remember the sound of your voice,
that one, at your most truest state,
the way you sounded in deep sleep at 3ish am something
how all of this will be so short lived.

–

And how stupid,
That on my way to see you off,
Every single time, each & every one!
How i still hold my tears & interchange them with a smile on
my lips
And then brainlessly think,
on my way back home,
Without you
that every single time out of those,
you must not have noticed the sobbing change in my tone.

–

But also how comforting,
That within all these days of distance
I still know, the joy of seeing you again is gonna be much
more bigger
And fulfilling

Than the time spent apart.

And how this interspace,

Was necessary

To get us close again,

& this time,

Closer than ever before.

You and me.

- Mishka B

203. The fault in our stars

Have you ever thought, this coming and going.

This meeting again and staying and then leaving.

This circle that we're placed in..

With love so unconditional, each time we meet with the same magnetic pull.

Like all that ever went wrong never existed.

And then we meet again and it goes wrong again.

And there we are thinking about each other.

And here I am, I can't help but think is it all a plot, like we're trapped in this conspiracy,

of the universe,

written in the stars.

A fault in our stars,

Maybe?

- Mishka B

204. Mulaqat

Roz khuda se maanga hai tumhe..

Har baar jab palak jhapki hai,

Apneaap ko tumme aur khota hua paya hai.

Aisa koi lamha nahi jab socha nahi,

Ye duniya jahan hum jee rahe hai,

Kaisi hoti agar hum saath hote??

Kya ek ek pal jo ghadi dekhkar katt raha hai,

Waisa hi hota?

Ya phir aisa jaise bijli,

Jo dekhi toh sahi par sunayi de tab tak us pal ko mehsoos hi
nahi kar payi.

Jaise vo lamha aate hi khatam hogaya.

–

Ye bhi sochti hoon ki jaise ghuma karte the yahan se vahan,

Befikar, bewajah

Kya agar aaj apne hi andar ghum loon

Toh jo thehraav mehsoos kiya tha tumhare saath,

Vo apne hi andar khoj paungi?

–

Sawaal toh hai, shayad jawaab bhi.

Lekin kuch jawaabo tak pohochna nahi chahti..

Kya pata shayad apneaap me tumse milte milte

Dobara haqeqat se waqif na hojau.

—

Ki kahin is duniya ke sookhepan se hamare saath ki geeli
zameen ko ek na kar doon.

—

Isiliye sab kuch wahin chodd ati hoon...

—

Ek aur baar,
Tumse milkar khali haath laut ati hoon..

————————

Ye bhi hua kabhi, jaise hua abhi..
Tujhko sabhi me paa liya.
- Mishka B

205. Phases of the moon

Every now & then, I think of you.

Think about the fact of how over the years I'm still unable to decide.

Decide & conclude. If you're miles & seas and oceans & planets & spaces away.

Or Are you still here. Like you used to be.

& are we still here. Like we used to be.

Holding on to each other like we did.

But with looser ends this time. Or maybe tangled ones. Our minds knowing no way out.

Just as one cannot figure out the start of a scribbled scratch work.

Does this mean we're closer to the end? Our end?

What about how we once used to define eternity then? Does that not exist anymore? Or has it faded or lost meaning or was it just a mirage we were unaware of? Whatever it be.

—

I think we're more like the moon

In phases we glow we grow we shine

And then we're complete.

But can we ever take no notice of what it means when we say-

We're still just "phases"

— of the moon

206. About the writer

About the writer :

Mishka B

.

.

Mishka loves to travel and is attracted to the spiritual nature
of things. She believes in old school form of the world,
bonfires and deep conversations. Her poems convey the
meaning of stars as she stargazes into reality.

207. An open letter to the person who would like to pen down our story

Hi,

There's a few things you're going to need to know about me if you're going to want to pen down a story with me. I am a paradoxical creature. I can be as stoic as an ultrasound technician who can see something wrong but won't react, and I can be as explosive as a fire cracker with the slightest provocation. I cannot fathom why this is, but THIS is who I am. I'm laying it bare right now, so that you know what you are in store for. I would never want you to feel like you are sailing an ocean which has been uncharted. I don't promise for the sailing to be the smoothest, but I promise you that this isn't the Bermuda Triangle.

The first time someone called me beautiful, I assumed it was a cruel joke. It left me feeling horrified and melancholic. Why would anyone call me something I'm not? Why would you taunt me like that? I know I'm not a marble statue. That's what is beautiful right? Their perfect proportions...the right curves...so why would you cruelly taunt me like that?

You don't get to call me beautiful. Not unless you can fall in love with my excessive curves, my glistening cinnamon skin, hurricane like soul, kaleidoscopic mind and child like need for affection. You don't get to call me beautiful if you can't trace your fingers on my skin and tell me that you've never felt more at home. And you most certainly do NOT get to call me beautiful, if all you're looking to do is slip me drops of cyanide through the crevices of my skin.

I know I probably ask for a lot, but this is who I am. And I will NEVER apologize for it.

So...are you ready to pen down our story?

- Nicole Urvi

208. Mould

I have the waves of the sea writ on my skin,
The brightest embers burning,
Thorns in the shape of goosebumps,
And ocean eyes filled with affection.
Yet for some reason,
I have never loved myself.
I have tried to break and pull at the Thorns,
Be rid of the waves,
And douse the embers.
All because I was told,
You can't be an all-in-one mould.
For years, I believed just that,
Until it finally broke upon me.
We are various kinds of aesthetic,
No matter what shape, color or quality.
I no longer feel the need to re-mould my mold.
Because my mould is what makes me pulchritudinous.
So here's to all of us, Figuring out,
How to love the waves writ on our skin,
Understanding the protection of the thorns
Fuelling the embers,
And drowning ourselves with affection.

- Nicole Urvi

209. 3:00 a.m.

It's 3:00 a.m.

While I desperately long for a kiss from nicotine,

It's been two weeks since I met her.

Chet Baker has been talking to me,

While the sound of the rotating fan,

Is as omni present as my breathing.

There's a wall covered in post-it notes.

Lines from books,

Words that have carved their space,

Messy doodles.

You see...I had a date tonight.

But, she was a no show.

I don't hold it against her though,

I never have.

She's always had issues with letting her walls down.

Because the moment she has gotten close,

She's seen them show up.

They charm their way through.

She wants to scream out loud that the charm is toxic,

But until the person realizes that she can't do nothing.

So I really don't hold anything against Sleep.

Especially because she has lost so many loved ones to insomnia.

- Nicole Urvi

210. About the Writer

About the Writer:

Nicole Urvi

Nicole Urvi is a 26 year old Social Worker from Kolkata. While she has done her MSW from IISWBM, her love for literature is what got her through to Jadavpur University in her undergrad. In her free time she loves to cook, write, listen to music, chill with her family and friends, and smash the patriarchy.

211. How I fell in love with grief

I saw grief coming tiptoeing towards me.
I felt like I was in a dream. He slowly held my waist and pulls me towards him and hugs me aggressively, I was gasping but it made my heart bloomed. As I closed my eyes and drowned in his embrace I felt divine. Echoes of his heartbeats repeat in my ears as if they are the most magical hymn anybody could ever create. He unfolds me, and witness a canvas painted with blood. He comes closer and wipes the extra blood that kept on dripping. The way his hands moved, unbothering my melancholy I felt safe, safer than ever. It made me want to contrive new emotions, where 24/7 I can write about him only him. Since that day I haven't stopped writing and my bedroom floor is a mess with all the poems and letters written in his name.

Now it's been 2months since I last saw him.He was taking the canvas with him and I didnt bother to ask him where he was heading to. I wish I did.
I can feel him in sleeping next to me whereas the bed is empty cold, I enchant all the love peoms till I sleep, by now I am addicted to grief even if it left me.

- Shrestha Dey

212. I still draw your portaits

You saw the moon sarcastically laughing at me for loving you but you said nothing. I saw you leapting from the balcony, your jeans getting torn near the knees and blood dripping. Still you went to her that night and I can't forget how at 9th standard you told me stories of her making you vulnerable, she thrusted her toxicity into you and you drank it all like it was fresh wine.

You smile looking at her and I draw portraits of you smiling. Everytime you spit her name out of your mouth I scratched my pen on the table, it almost has a hole now.

Every evening when you walked 2 steps I walked 4 to save you from falling in the same manhole and you just smiled and said I know you the best. I don't want that. All I want from you is to inject your love in my skin slow and all. I want you to stare deep into my soul and make the desert inside me fill with love.

You put your head in my lap and sleep, most of the afternoons pass this way and she hates me more for this but the fake smile she puts on doesn't hide her jealous fragrance that she is wearing. I want to hate her so much but everytime she breaths I know your breath is hitched with her.

On some days my empty inside makes me collapse in the glum bathroom floor, the hazy cold showers still manages to makes my body burn.

I get up with red eyes read all those songs you wrote in a diary that now is lost,(I stole it) I know those are written about me because she would never admire white flowers and grief. I am the one who drinks her lover's sad stories and feels contented. I am the one who stitches her heart every night to see her lover's heart bloom in heavens garden. I know that you know how much I die for you every full moon night but still take no notice of how I've made you my religion.

- Shrestha Dey

213. 4 spring passed

Mother described me to her friends as a quite girl who used to sit alone in one corner of her class but rather I was a girl full of rage wanted to spit unspoken words dipped in guilt.

I never showed those poems inked beneath my skin to them, poems of love and disguise. The pain in my throat cripples and stupefy me. I inherited the curse of loving the ones who will never love me back and each night I let my body burn like wildfire.

4 springs elapsed since I last saw you, your smile still etched in my ribs gave birth to crying butterflies. I still remember how every night you used to visit me with grief clinging onto you and I could not resist your green eyes that promised me 365moonlit nights.

By the midnight you imprinted sweet kisses dripping like honey from your lips to mine. The winds letting the curtains to curl up softly.

This room was filled with delusional romance, paper seaming hearts ready to tear apart, unknowingly feeding pain to unverified love.

The wrinkles in my forehead already forecasted how this night was the last that we were side by side.

But I was happy in my misery, atleast I saw constellations in your eyes and moonlit nights were still a dream I could carry along for the rest of my life.

- Shrestha Dey

214. Mum do you know?

Mum, I know I have never been this quite but believe me I want to share what's wrong with me but my tongue feels so heavy and lips glued that I just can't. I only know that my heart keeps rotting away in someone else's backyard.

Out of 26 alphabets you taught me, 4 are missing which makes up his name and I don't think I can complete my sentence without those 4. I don't sleep at night and bleed from eyes, eyes are anyway meaningless because I am too blinded by him. My skul doesn't bloom with pretty pink flowers and I can hardly get drunk on grief. Everything is weirdly normal around me but why am I being so mean. I stab myself and it actually feels great but I don't die. My blood instead gets lump and creates new branches of me. Mum I know you saw me almost die near the old lake but I survived. You didn't say anything and hugged me, are you still angry because I went out of house without telling you.

Mum, dad doesn't Come home often and my step sister told my classmates that I am nothing more than some badly sculptured bones that doesn't fit well and stink like dead animals that crows are afraid to eat. But I really don't. I smell normal. Don't I?

- Shrestha Dey

215. About the Writer

About the Writer:

Shrestha Dey

Shrestha is an Aesthete person who highly believes in platonic love and like to chase sunsets. To her writing is like drawing grief onto canvas.

216. Hero-lovers

We are visual animals. So much so that we also want to see love. Point in case: Their face. Everything about love is invisible, but our minds make us believe that it's the visual we are in love with. Her face, her eyes, her smile, her frown, the rolling of her eyes, her beautiful neck. Hot priest's beautiful neck. Love is fragmented in these little visual perks.

All memories of love are visually stored, not in our brains but also in memorabilia, photos, and social media. I see my hand holding hers. As I sit behind her on her scooty, I see the city, my face uncomfortably placed on her shoulder. The city appears to be in a hurry. I am reminded of the various heroes of hindi cinema that have been seen on screen, running on these city streets for their love. The lover-heroes are in a hurry. All love is served to us through popular cinema on a visual platter of spectacle and affect. In mobilising scopophilic desire, cinema taught us to 'see' love. No wonder holding gaze is a turn-on. We love the lover-hero, he teaches us to love. We love the lovers; the lovers love us back. There is nothing invisible here, we are told. Everything that is evident, is evidence, is visible. Well, what about the invisible then?

We have all the invisible things that our love is made of. Her voice, her breath, her khusboo, the khusboo of her breath. The weight of her head on my chest, her soft skin, her touch is freakishly soft, almost fragile. Can I touch her back? But I do not want to hurt her. Through countless hesitations, miles on eggshells, we become one, ossified.

Things that are felt, not seen.

The first fluterrings of butterflies, the softening of walls that took years to build. The visual heart - not the bloody, biological one that runs our body - is seen exercising its muscles. The blossoming of flowers on the interstices of what's real and not, the sprightly expansion of our horizons - of what can be believed and how much, is not seen. The flooding inside your heart, of the beloved's most choked gutters through those broken walls.

A tight slap, that the lover-hero strikes 'his' woman with, is visible, is seen. She is seen fallen; she is seen crying. Her tears, visible. What burst, exploded inside her, what broke, what birthed inside her - it could easily contain the sun - that is not seen. We are visual animals, animals. Animals.

- Seher

217. Fall

Why do leaves fall?
Just like the season,
the phenomenon of falling of leaves is
warm and melancholic
Wonder if
it's an act
Nature trying to tell you and me
That it cries too,
that it too falls
with me
with you
is it the way nature
holds our hands?

- Seher

218. Satan wears red lipstick

What makes red enticing?
Fully red lips and fully red fruit run red parallelly
Passion, love, blood, violence
are all so dependent on red
for representation
We are born in red goo and red piss
Nasha comes red in wine
Water is red in some kinds of watermelons
It's what satan wears

- Seher

219. About the Writer

About the Writer:

Shraddha Sharma (Pen name Seher)

Seher has written for catharsis but she now only writes to glide. She loves food, tending to plants, and creating art in whatever medium possible.

220. // info //

EVERGREEN DIARY

We started the Evergreen Diary project when we noticed many writers, every year, go unnoticed for their hard work and creativity. One of our goals is to provide them a platform through which they can showcase their talent along with a moral high ground for support.

—

Visit www.evergreendiary.com for more info.
Thank you to all the selected writers and for your support!

Printed by Libri Plureos GmbH in Hamburg, Germany